Rugs On Puddles
Coats Over Oceans

Poems & Lyric Poetry
by
K.A. Schultz

Kimann Schultz

Rugs on Puddles Coats Over Oceans

Poems & Lyric Poetry by K.A. Schultz

Dakeha Taunus LLC, publisher Copyright 2024 by K.A. Schultz

ALL RIGHTS RESERVED

RUGS ON PUDDLES COATS OVER OCEANS is a collection of works of poetry. Resemblances to actual people, living or dead, places or events, can be coincidental.
No AI was used in the creation or execution of this literary work.

No work herein may be re-posted or reproduced, stored in a retrieval system, or transmitted in any manner without the express written consent of K.A. Schultz & Dakeha Taunus LLC

Inquiries may be addressed to kimannschultz@gmail.com

Cover art by K.A. Schultz

https://linktr.ee/K.A.Schultz & www.butterflybroth.com

Amazon paperback ISBN 978-0-9824229-2-2

The poems and lyrics found herein were written
over the course of over twenty years
1991-2011 and 2012, 2013
And continue to be edited

Dates of origin are noted, as are dates or years of edits

All lyric poems exist as fully realized songs, written
and recorded with Michael L. Schultz

A sampling of songs can be found at
at Amazon.com, at iTunes and on YouTube

Table of Contents

I. The Recognition of a Certain Wisdom –
   Some Call it Growing Up

1.	Friends
2.	Trust
3.	Well-Being
4.	Fear
5.	Longing
6.	Emerging
7.	Hyperexistence
8.	Kaleidoscopic View
9.	A Picnic, No
10.	Jacqueline
11.	Live It Up
12.	As I Fly
13.	How To Get There
14.	Mirrors
15.	Shine On
16.	Better Stuff
17.	Love I & II

II. The Universal Diminutive, Definitive

1. My Angels in Red Suits
2. Little Answers
3. Treasure
4. David
5. Stop
6. Chance
7. On Tears by Daniel Z Ellis
8. November
9. Making Love
10. Sorry
11. 'tis Time to Go
12. Cold Coffee
13. I'm so Smart, etc
14. The Tired Lady Admits
15. The Excitable Boy Invites
16. Cooling
17. Audiowhat
18. No More Angels
19. Prayer
20. Conch Shell by Hannah M Schultz
21. Early Spring by Hannah M Schultz
22. Daisies & Daffodils by Hannah M Schultz

III. The Losing and the Gaining

1. You Said
2. What You Said
3. The Unsaid
4. Freedom I
5. Freedom II
6. Round & Round & Round
7. Ain't it a Damn Shame
8. The Before and the After
9. New Heart
10. Bittersweet
11. In the Midnight of Your Leaving
12. Face to Face
13. Little Bitters
14. Daniel and Kevin
15. Daniel
16. We Know

IV. The Incidental and the Awakening

1. My Own Time
2. Breathe (My Own Time II)
3. Untasted
4. In the Gallery
5. Who Are You?
6. Save Me
7. Aperitif
8. Appetite
9. Back to You
10. I am Strong Enough to Catch You
11. I Can Wait
12. Forever Is Allowed
13. Street of Dreams
14. 1992
15. Close in the Distance
16. Distraction
17. You Got Me
18. Ever Since
19. In A Wake
20. Watercolor Words

V. *The Redefining of Love*

1. Here I am
2. I Do
3. The Redefining of Love
4. Chrysalis
5. That Line
6. The Landscape of Your Love
7. You Ask
8. Healing Kisses
9. I'm Sorry
10. Joy
11. Close to Far Away
12. My Walk
13. Your Voice, Your Song
14. Waiting, Waiting
15. I'm Here
16. The First of Love
17. Marking Time
18. Play Me
19. Terms
20. Is There?
21. A Man, Two Boys
22. Exodus/Genesis
23. The Place of All Senses
24. Life Imitates Art
25. Breathe Me

VI. Rugs on Puddles/Coats Over Oceans

1. Our Lady
2. Your Name
3. Rugs on Puddles/Coats over Oceans
4. Autumn's Fall
5. And Why do I Hold On?
6. Turn Turn
7. Coarse Vespers
8. Black Box
9. Monarchs
10. The Banner of Her Love
11. I Want to Die a King (The Money Pit)
12. Coins to Close His Eyes
13. Jane
14. Hell-Bent to Heaven
15. She Wants
16. A Scorching Kind of Cool
17. The Monster
18. Hand Over Fist
19. The Hancock Red
20. Citizens and Fools
21. A Bluer Shade of Blue
22. Iron Clad
23. Isle of Unknown
24. Ode to Cooperian Ideal
25. Raindance
26. Ode to Magellan
27. Xmas
28. Donkey-Hohtey
29. *The Loft*

VII.   Studio E – the Lyrics

1. Spirit of Christmas – the poem
2. Spirit of Christmas – the carol
3. Spirit of Christmas – revisited
4. Life Steps In
5. Lullabye – Ship of Dreams
6. Imagine Me With You
7. Pirouette
8. Everyone
9. Gun Metal Ghost
10. Another Way of Dying
11. Elle 'Dora
12. Hiyalaya
13. Hymn to Her – the poem
14. Hymn to Her – the song
15. 8-2-Midnight
16. The Crazy I Could Be
17. I Like These Kinds of Blues
18. "Play Chicago"
19. Forget About Me
20. The Haunting
21. Don't
22. Name this Hurricane
23. Eclipse
24. Come, Child, Katie
25. Though I Had Nearly Forgotten You – the poem
26. Though I Had Nearly Forgotten You – the song
27. It's OK – the poem
28. Is it Okay – the song, by MLS
29. Ladders
30. Noble Little Soldier
31. Pendulum is Rising
32. Art
33. Words
34. Sleepless
35. Tonight, I'll be in Heaven
36. Earthbound Ethereal
37. Beautiful Rage, draft

38.   Beautiful Rage, with coda

DEDICATION

I like it when the light recedes
When day wanes
And night beckons
And habitual traffic gives way to paths less charted
I like it when the dark is near

I think my eyes are failing me
As sure as the years are hailing me
The sun is crass
And overrated
By shadows caressed
The stark evaded
I prefer the bulb
The flame
The screen illuminated
Attendant to my hov'ring hands
In that momentary, pregnant pause
Before tomes
And poems are vented
Rendered from the gut, the endocept
Made firm to stand against
A firmament
Filled with non-readers
Non-seekers
Haters
Believers

Dogma may once have burned
To heart
To sage
Unfortunate mankind-kindled ages
With Fate's scissors turned and trimmed
To air
To dust
To selective memory and complacence
The victor, for worse or for the better,
Takes by force the privilege,

It is he who turns the pages

I'll do lyrics
And verses
And stories and studies
In prayerful, audacious literary homage
To Dickens and his purpose and his beauteous narratives
So that the chains which bind me
(And all that I will ever leave undone)
To this earth and my paltry place in time
Will not forever drag on and on
Nor forever drag me down.

May my words,
To mine who know me yet not,
Redeem me, place me, and seal me.

3-5-2012/2-14-2013

I. The Recognition of a Certain Wisdom – Some Call it Growing Up

FRIENDS

A bridge for whispers,
Sighs and tears
Tell me all of your worries
Tell me all of your fears
You know
There's always laughter
In the long after
Though what we feel at times
Is traced as if carved into ancient stone
Paths and patterns on bouldered walls
Fabric we're taught to call happiness
Threadbare tapestries we call memories
Woven in silk and gut and blood and ashes
Warped by life's companion sadness

In the understanding
We fathom color
In the questionning
We embrace the shadows
And arrive at last at knowledge
The enhancing lies in the shrugging off
Of any stones that weigh us down

We feel,
After all,
Because we are alive.
Because we are friends,
We share.

2-7-92/2009/2011/2-14-2013

TRUST

Let me go
And see me coming back to you.
The curve of your smile
The arc of your arms
Are like the horizons of a love
That is worth attempting
In you,
I'm free
So let me go

Let me go
And see me coming back to you.

12-91/2009

WELL-BEING

Everything is as it should be
I feel a passionate kind of peace
That surges gently through my being
I see it all within your eyes
I want to feel the hurricane
And name it after you.

2-12-92

FEAR

There's no more Land of Oz
There's no more Neverland
I'm standing in an empty room
My arms rest idly above languid hands
The fine line between lonely
And all alone
Grows less and less and less defined
And my feet feel as if fused to the ground
Did I forget to fly?

Be a part of me
As an energy
As something with which to overcome
Whatever
As you are handed over
In your infinite incarnations
Time and time and time again
Be it quicksand hills or emotions' abysses
Remind me to look both ways
But let me cross
And see me on

1992/2009/2011/2-14-2013

LONGING

I thought my search was over
I thought you'd found me, too
I thought my dreams had once come true
I hoped I'd found my home in you
I thought the dream-like love at night
Would still be there with morning light
But, like the night, chased by the sun,
My wish was taken just in fun
How i wish you'd been the one
How i wish you'd been the one
How i wish you'd been the one

1992

EMERGING

The shoes on the hearth are mine
But they don't fit me anymore
I outgrew them years ago
The cords and ties that bound
Unraveled in the wind
They're streamers now
Free to catch and hold the breeze
That takes and holds each wayward kite
You once helped me hold me there
But I've been carried on to other skies
Your horizons never knew.

It's not that I am leaving you
I'll always be a part of you
I'm now just me
Who I am is not *just* me
I'm *me*
And I'm going to be just fine.

I'm a woman now
Sometimes I even think I'm beautiful
I thank you for the best you gave
As for the rest,
From a context flawed,
I know how hard you tried
I believe I understand.

In the best of love
We are set free
So take my word,
Believe in me
I'm not *just* me
I'm *me*
And I'm going to be just fine.

1992/2009/2-14-2013

HYPEREXISTENCE

That, when the souls
Have already been joined
The bodies then must meet
Such passion leaves no aftertaste
Its essence lingers sweet

No games, no ego
To mar the cadence
When, hand in hand
Just a look
Can put the universe into a nutshell.

1991-92/2011

KALEIDOSCOPIC VIEW

Don't lose
The kaleidoscopic view
Our music lends
The day to day may seem small and plain
Compared to the vastness of a song
Hold on
Soon it will be yours, perhaps someday as ours
A ball of fire
Larger than the sun
Will settle and become
The lamp that lights the notes
Your voice will stir the flame
I play silent harmony as I watch
Your ordinary muse
I will
Urge you on
Give you somehow
The gift of better than before.

You have blessed me with that power
And built a temple in a basement cell
What a lovely, love-filled world
Four small walls, a floor, a ceiling make
You sing
I listen
And then we write some more
_ ___ ___.
You know the words.

3-92

A PICNIC, NO

No one said I'd have a picnic
When the blanket was laid out
No one said it'd be a party
When my first-born son cried out
A picnic, no,
My precious spuds are sometimes beasts
A picnic, no,
But so much more
They are a feast.

1992

JACQUELINE

Jacqueline,
Don't these damn roads
Get longer every day
Don't mirages bend our sight
And best intentions end in fight
Pieces of wisdom
Scraps of faith
You're living in an age of blue-plate philosophy
And even though you want to give
You're forced to get what you can take.

Oh, Jacqueline,
What's honesty
Who's understanding who
Are the talks we've had enough
To elevate our well-meant thoughts
Pieces of wisdom
Scraps of faith
You're looking for chivalry on a bed-bent date
And what you used to read of love
Is just too hard to re-create
In these modern days
In these modern ways…

Jacqueline,
You can smile for me if you want to
But you don't have to
You can be strong for me
But you don't have to
You can be wise and erudite for me
And I will understand
If even that prescription skips a beat
And the mask of maturity slips a bit
For we are friends
Two frightened little girls
A pair of savvy bitches
Funded by the precious exchange

Of our fragile, searching selves
We can feel and cut and live to talk about it
Even if it hurts,
Even when it hurts.

Oh, Jacqueline,
Best intentions
Entrenched in chimeric ambition:
Things that used to be
Things that never were
Things you want that will never be
Things best left alone
Pieces of wisdom
Scraps of faith
I hope you find some truth inside of your cheery intervention
And that your reflection smiles back at you
When no one else is in the room
In a moment void of all pretense.

5-22-92/2009/2011/2012

LIVE IT UP

Whatever lights your candle
Whatever floats your boat
Whatever strikes your fancy
Whatever gets your goat
This play on words
This world we play upon
These sing-song words
These words to which we sing along
That sweetest of love's arching songs
The gods of love with arrows won.

They can't be wrong
If music makes it with a song
You pack it in and take along
The life you live that grants each day
The one life you'd live anyway
For all our freedoms
We are equally choiceless
You like to live, or so you say…
So forge ahead, away, away

Bring it, bring it, bring it on
Come on in and come on up
Take it, take out, take it up
Shout it up and shout it out
Shout it out and oh, so loud
Sing it every single day
And keep these words that I now say
For I love to take no more from you
Than you would dare to hold me to.

Whatever brings the bacon
Whatever turns you on
Whatever hay you tumble
When half-baked, best-laid cookies crumble
This world of rules
This game whose rules

We step on, pounce on, break in two
The broken rules we dance around
Excuses, ruses, fables, foils
A glass shard littered playing ground
On shining lies we gamblers bank
Like fish too soon are hooked thereon.

These melodies
These rhythms, these rhymes
These sounds we love, are blinded by
And turned from by a deafened ear
When it no longer suits us
Like the rumor that life's just a myth
And reality enboxed
It's nothing more than gray-scale eggshells
One inside the other
Yet, when it's through, we fight it off,
Kicking, screaming, push it off
A naked, shivering, foolish youth
Who, hungry, only asks for more.

I can't be wrong
If music makes it with a song
You pack it in and take along
The all night-long
The all day-long
The life you live, your life each day
The choices choose *you* every day
As beggars choose, we've not much say…
Although otherwise we all assume

So, rue it
Tune it
Turn it on
Turn it on and turn it up
Live it, live on, live it up
On and up
And faster, higher
'til cradled like an earthbound flyer

In the stratosphere thus blanketed
At last
At last, one wish is granted
That once and for forevermore
Everything to be is just the way
It should for now and forever be

Oh, I am having fun with this
And hope that you are too,
For fun is what will keep me young
At least 'til I grow old.

Give in, give it
Give it up
Live on, live it
Live it up
Up and out
And out and over
And over and over and over and over
The whole night day-long dipthong through
So are you having fun here too?
'cause I am having fun with you
And fun is how the end effect
Affects us in the end.

1989/92/2009/2011/2012/2-14-2013

AS I FLY

As I fly
The freedom to be me
Alone
Exists
As I let my feelings go
To rise above the norms
And step beyond these walls
A peacefulness envelopes me
As tattered cloaks of purpose fall

The inner me
Forsakes pretense
My soul extends
Beyond my mediocre frame
A thought flies borne
Of no defense
I'm laughing at the sky

I like the view
This distance lends
I see the earth
So softly bend
It turns
In time
The days go by
Becomes the night
Give way to light
One time,
One time
Then once again, completed

The thin, cold air
Blows through my hair
I see my hands
Outlined against the dark
Simple forms
Work bent

They've served me well
What's now to come
I cannot tell
I only know
As I see here
The ordinary roles we play
Can't take you where
You really, really want to be
For ought to overrides
The desperate longing to
To be, be, be

If you could only see
As I can't help but see
This error-ridden comedy
The charades we're forced to play
And the characters we have built
And how it all soon fades
And too soon dims on down to black
The way I understand it now
Is that heaven's laughter echoes
With indifference
Not indulgence
Nor with centrist, idyllic interference;
Tomorrow we are forgotten

And that somehow, this has to be all right.

As I fly
I soar
Through countless nights
Dark constellations
Punctuated with ten-thousand questions
And solitary people wondering
Who's with whom tonight.

I pray
For peace
And for serenity

I pray
For love that gives
And takes accordingly
And lasts forever,
Amen.

1991/2009/2011/2012/2-14-2013

HOW TO GET THERE

If I wanted the sun
Should I at least be shooting for the moon?
Should I outfit my little gray ghost with a quiver
Of recycled forks
To carry as messenger the puny arrows
With which to pierce the cold, dead hearts
Of whichever petrified body
Is discovered slumbering in its path
(in fear or slothful homage)?
I do not, I have not
I want all of this so bad
I see a future
A clear, virginal pool
Coagulated in a cave
Of a thousand million years or more
Peopled with the eyeless, the unevolved
Content in all they do not know
The blissful, yes indeed!
Therein lies an edge
Out of which I must somehow crawl
One, two, three….

The landscape is a quilt of innocence
Covered in a numbing snow
Soothed, smoothed over
Inquiries blanketed by comfort zones

I won't mind
If bats and mice
Devour the trail mix I leave in my wake
Should one long to return from wence one came?
And when is from wence one came no longer that thing called home?

Once the pool is found,
I will search and seek
Until I have memorized

What mesmerized
Then, even if on hands and knees,
I'll know how to get there.

6-18-92/2009/2011/2012/2-14-2013

MIRRORS

I'm trying to make waves
To leave some sort of mark
I want to tell the future's past
"I am here!"
I want to see (I must confess)
My name within the stars
To cause a skip in time's infernal, endless line
Some little thing historians can one day identify
And make some insignificant bit of prose
End sweetly with a bit of rhyme

Give me pages to write on
Give me instruments to play
Give me just enough encouragement
To look beyond the day
Listen to me, listen
My cloth turns into circles, circles
There are, I hope, mirrors in these granite walls
Illuminated long and dark and narrow halls

How would you ever notice me
From your lofty, lovely, little space?
I could be everything
You would ever want
We could be so complete
So much better when lived on in sum
Do not underestimate
The strength in follies' middle names
Creation's just a godly game
Played to the death until, one day,
Insanity overtakes
And with masterpieces is replaced
What depths lie in a drunken sailor's Luna Sea
When only halting echos answer back
The distracted yeoman navigates
And crashes, lust-filled, mistaken

I know you're being faithful
To the promise in all those good intentions
You are there, and
You are there
Just beyond this mortal's reach
The essence of a dreamer's dreams
Requires that I jump
But I can catch us if the two of us
In tandem choose to fall
But recognize how small, how small
I am
You are
As am I
Or so we seem against the endless backdrop
Of this unsung, matted, sunless sky
That is bound by endless, lying eights
That lie forever in weighted wait
Is this the metronome?

Let's dance and ask for rain or storms
And peer beyond all measured time
Let's dare the heat to sap our reach
And pull where it may take us

Create for me an ocean blue
Where silent deserts lay dead before
I'll be your artist, faith restored
You write a story, then tell me
Our history
Will be
The best one written
So far.

6-92/2009/2011/2012/2-14-2013

SHINE ON

When to let go
I don't know, I don't know
I only hope the answers
Present themselves
As easily as the dawn begins its day
I only hope it's easy
Enough to say good-bye
You will reflect the best of me
For I gave you what I could
Shine on, my sun
Shine on, my son

Shine through those dreary, friendless days
Shine in your quiet, stoic way
Time is yet your friend
And circumstance is on your side
Though it'll take decrepit age to know this
You're going to do just fine

Where to begin
Who's to tell
I can't say
I only hope the stories
That I told you then
Hold true to their noblest of definitions
I was your faulted but well-meant teacher
Trial and error in my Sunday best
Now keep with you whatever's left
I showed you what I could
I showed you light as I understood it
So shine on, my sun
Shine on, shine on, my son

No, I rather you didn't cry
Would prefer you didn't look inside
My heart will do its own thing
Horizons call your name

Echoes repeat the same
Whatever you do will be the first page
Of a rudimentary but grand epistle
Bound by thoughts and feelings
Made boundless by your questions
Be sure to leave an unsung space
Where wisdom can yet write between your lines
Listen to its silence
Hear the things you won't talk about
Invite the things you won't understand
But know
Die Sonne bringt es an den Tag
So shine on my sun,
Shine on, my child
Shine on, shine on, my son.

5-27-92/2011/2012/2-14-2013

BETTER STUFF

I am made up
Of better stuff than you
Your childhood hurts
Your chains and leaden weights
Cannot be paid forward
By your outstretched, angry hand
I will deflect you
As I have done so all my days
With the I of me and I am calm
I am
Made up of
Better stuff than you

I am graced with
Potential of my choosing
Your ceilings, basements
Closets, gravestones
Cannot, cannot define me
In a context only you would recognize
Or hold dear
By virtue of its similarity to you
Your selfish, flawed, forsaken self
With my eyes I see and I am calm
I am
Made up of
Better stuff than you

And I am beautiful
Though you have never told me so
I have crafted this
By heartfelt thought and task
And with what looks back at me
Each time I look into the glass
Each time I look into the past
Mine is an ever hopeful, shaky sun
That appeases
Makes up for

All that came from you
I am
Made up of
Better stuff than you

I am made up
Of words that have been washed away
And all misguided legacy
I would not have be mine
I've thrown my body
Beyond the shadow of your tree
And trusted in the balm of time
I have redefined

It's better stuff
That calls me
It's better stuff
Which beckons
It's better stuff
That holds me
And cradles
Face in warmest hands
Oh see, sister Fate
She has seen fit
To pull me on and on and on and on
She holds my face
In withered hands
Wills me, dares me, "Smile back!"
By word and deed
I smile back
By song and tale
I smile back
By rung, by step
I smile back
By forward leap
I smile back

Back or forth
Forward and Back

The spiral, though it tries me
Brooks the dry field and seeks the sea
I am its willing trav'ler

3-23-12/2-14-13

LOVE I & II

Love I
Is conditional
But it is of the fountain from which I wish to remain
Thirsty forevermore
Your taste is sweet and it suits me
Now as it did then
It is an agreement
To respect enough to not want pain
To be reflected by word or deed
In the heart or soul of the other
The book I wish to write with you
Grows from word to page to chapter to volume
As do the rooms we build to hold them
Let me wake anew and be thankful
That it is your face a few inches from mine
For each day as it starts anew
For each day as it dies, as I know we must, some day, too
May we time that in good cadence with each other
May we always, a little, miss each other
May we love so that our love teaches
Those we love best
To love another even better

Love II
May my love inspire
Me to be a me
That, if some day, you see some trace
In the face of the magic you will, I hope, someday have wrought
You are pleased and not disappointed
You feel connected, not unfortunately bound
So that, if thus reminded, you can smile
And that it is a good thing.
May you love beyond anything I could have loved
May you be loved more than I was ever loved
May you move beyond any inevitable hurt that comes your way
May you be more beautiful than I could ever have been

May you be more talented than anything I could ever have crafted
with my own hand
May you go farther than I will have ever travelled
May you understand and forgive all I did not do correctly
(this wisdom lands only in the aftermath)
May you hold in the deep spaces of your heart the memories
So that when you think back on me
You not only love or dutifully honor me
But *like* the foundation that was your mother

2-15-2013

II. The Universal, Diminutive, Definitive

MY ANGELS IN RED SUITS

Like Christmas Eve
I pray for one blessed silent night
I pray for help to face their eager faces
Come the first rays of each morning's light

Those two tornadoes
Those tiny locomotives
Yes, they're mine
Lord bless me and help me at the same time
I've heard it said
The grass is always greener
On the other side
Those who have, they want
Those who want, have not
I've got my boys
Two babes from heaven sent
Two hundred diapers, what a scent
Two thousand tears, tiny egos bent
Before too long
I'll look both ways
And wonder where it went.

1991

LITTLE ANSWERS

Little answers to my prayers
Sleeping in their beds upstairs
May the stars in heaven watch them close
When I cannot be there
For, in spite of me
Every bit of me
Loves my little answers so.

1991

TREASURE

I've been a miner
And I've dug deep and low
I've worked my fingers to the bone
But, yet, this rock-hard mother earth
Resists with all my very search
While vultures watch
From their far-off perch
And remember they forgot their lunch.

1991/2009

DAVID

I like the endings
Where shepherds become heroes.

1992

STOP

Did you ever blink your eyes and find
The comet's trail fade to the night
And sigh
And think
The loss was small
Small lights, like freckles in the sky
As stars
More vast, more distant, so far beyond
Anything the small mind dares fathom
How can anyone imagine
Just how big
They really, really are?
So, go ahead
And smell the flowers
The sneeze will do you good.
It did,
After all,
Work for Scrooge.

4-92/2009/2011

CHANCE

There are two sides to each coin
Can't we carry fortunes, then
Fortune tellers, no, we're not
All we see is what we've got
We're left with no more, but not with less
Than the pittance we're wont to hold
To our hollow breasts
We leave the rest to crease the brow
And sigh to signal our collective weariness
Let's not question anything
Anymore
No more, no less;
No more

Acceptance of the inevitability
Of all
As being wrought
Of heads or tails
Has to be all right
Because that is how things fall.

1991/4-92/2011/2012

ON TEARS

Every kind of feeling
Is in every tear
It floats up out of your heart
And up your nose
And into your brain
And when it comes out of your eye
You can see it
And you remember it
It's kind of like a travelling system
I once ate my tear
And it tasted salty
Mom, why is there salt in our tears?

11-30-92
Daniel Z. Ellis
6 years old

TO MY SON IN AFGHANISTAN

Merry day to you
Whatever day it may be
Safe sleep
Happy dreams
      Of cute girls
      Cheesy pizzas
Guardian protected patrols
      Force fields of love
      Force fields of positive thoughts
Wide-eyed wakeful alertness
      Eyes out in front
      Eyes at your back
      Open hearts and healing
Welcome in 2010
And we'll start counting the days down
Until we meet you
With hugs and a kiss
And a frosty cold one for your thirst.

xoxoxomomxoxoxo
12/2009

NOVEMBER

Time hangs on trees
Days melt and stain the leaves
The speed of light is much too slow
Just watch the canvas go
When winter's weary monochrome
Comes only in shades of cold,
So cold
The night outweighs the day
The day
And snow collides with rain.
And snow collides with rain.

1992

MAKING LOVE

In the midst of love's confusion
Is it fission, is it fusion
Does one body really end
Where the other one begins?

12-92

SORRY

Sorry is just 5 letters long
5 smart, small letters can't be that wrong.

12-92/2009

'TIS TIME TO GO

When it's come that far
That every moment between
Every now and then
That has ever, ever been
Is no more reason enough to stay
Methinks, 'tis time to go.

12-92/2009

COLD COFFEE

You are like cold coffee
Left too long on the table
In a crack-handled cup
I no longer want to keep
Let me sleep.

3-92

I'M SO SMART

Synapse's a snap
When your mind's as sharp
As a whip
A snap's only as sweet
As the proximity
Of a tongue
To a licorice whip
Oh please.

I find myself in a dark hall
A theatre built of dreams
The silver screen is a folded sheet
That covered once the marriage bed
Then, when everything was said and done
And in anger once more undone
The bed became a playing field
An empty field of dreams.

Just one more thing
He said
Just go away
She thought
Did you ever…
No, I haven't…
Feel any sadness at this thing
The pain left long ago
That's when I knew it was over…
Ok
Sorry I asked…
Don't be…
See you…
Good-bye…

I anticipate the wait
Already eased into warmth
To see your smile beyond the lace

Then to feel your kisses on my face.

Thought-spun haiku
Little words
Intended to encompass
All this love
All the littleness of the knowledge
We aspire to attribute to wisdom
Hell, we learn.

You are the sleepy-eyed child
Pre-dawn awakened on a Christmas morn'
I am the package
In passion en-wrapped
Waiting
To be opened.

3-1992/2010

THE TIRED LADY ADMITS

I used to be
Your cup of tea
But now you get
Just dregs of me.

1992

THE EXCITABLE BOY INVITES

My electric blue Superior
With the hot pink leather interior
Come on babe, why don't we go
And I'll show you my dominoes.

1992

COOLING

What should have been forever
Becomes most likely never
Dust settles on my love
Dust settles on my love.

1992

AUDIOWHAT

Audiowhat
Sound to slap silly the silence
Let stoic peace and quiet be deluged
With cracks and sparks of tone
Beat and heartbeat harmonize
In cadence and in confusion married
To words the shadow dwellers write
Pictures and novels
Plays and epic stories
The universe, the acorn
Renderings, meanderings
Rememberings, forgettings…

…three verses,
A bridge,
Refrain,
Refrain;
refrain, refrain,
The end.

9-22-92/2009

NO MORE ANGELS

It shimmers like a burst of stars
The shimmers you can't feel
But why the baby's pain-filled tears
Do anything but heal
Do we need to make more angels
Are not the heavens full enough
Why cannot all this energy
Be used as power could in love?

The little girl in Russia
Spoke words I could not know
Yet when she cried
She sounded just like one of mine
My child's tears shine, too.

They're angels
Let us keep them with us
On an earth alive with green and blue
Not black and sick and self-consumed.

They're angels
Let us guide them towards the wisdom we yet lack
And lead them to the answers we still seek
Let's not leave them with nothing more
Than all the questions we are still
Forced like imbeciles to keep.

They're angels
Let each and every last one of them
 Re-write the pages in their own hand
And let them call each new truth their own
Pages not consumed by fire
Words borne of an evolved desire
And mankind's promise held intact.

They're angels
My God, just let them be

Their innocence ranks superior,
For as children,
They can be the real believers.

1991/2009/2011/2012

PRAYER

Lord, don't you know
I'm crying somewhere
Every minute, every hour
And my heart,
Lord, don't you know
Despite best efforts
Is still not made of stone
It has melted like the snow
With the heat of a lust for life I cannot help but feel
I'm creeping onto every shore
The water's edge that licks at me
Leaves me wanting
Wanting more
Feeling enough
To see the black
That closely, oh so closely
Nips at the heels of
A virgin's tight-lipped white.

I reach to kiss the moon
And cradle the sun
Like a child's upturned face
My deepest arms embrace delight
My valleys grip the shadowed night
And Earth, she sings
Listen!
She sighs
Her echoes shout redundantly
Forgiven, you are forgiven
Her voices cry
Can't you let each other be?
Freedom bends the saddened brow
As soldiers tear each other down
And consider it a job well done.

They tear each other down
And hell's a party just begun

Fed with hate and destructive desires
In hell a party's going on
Each man composes his invitation
And carves it in his breast
Tough guys
Lovers, infants, sons
Each one is someone else's child.

All I am looking for is a little love
And some small insight into happiness
And that it
Whatever It may be
Spreads like disease or wildfire
And kills of every decibel of that which is not of song.
That's all.

1992/2010/2011/2012

CONCH SHELL

Conch shell, you're smooth as silk
Conch shell, oh, conch shell
You're bright as morning light.
People would have to look at you
Before they see how bright.
Conch shell, you're yellow and you're gold
You're super bright as morning light.
You're yellow and you're gold.
Your sound of waves is impeccable.
I dare to take a sight.

Hannah Madison Schultz
Age 7
2010-2011 in-class poetry writing
Transposed to print with spelling and line placement edits by Kimann

EARLY SPRING

Early Spring is wonderful.
The snowflakes dance and diddle.
Oh, wily Spring
Oh, wily Spring
How I love you so.
Oh, your beautiful snow flake
Your wonderful breeze
Your beautiful flowers
And lovely moon
How lovely is your sun
You must see the joy of Nature
To see the beauty of early Spring.

Hannah Madison Schultz
Age 7
2010-2011 in-class poetry writing
Haiku (as noted on her original paper)
Transposed to print with spelling and line placement edits by Kimann

DAISIES & DAFFODILS

Daisies and Daffodils
Swinging around
I think they look like a beehive swinging around
Don't you?
I think they look like me!

BABIES & FABIES

Babies and fabies all lined in a row
All mixed together on the ground
Swinging around

FISHES & WISHES

Fishes and wishes
All together singing
So wishes all over the world
Will make all wishes come true

RAGS & FLAGS

Rags and flags
All lined in a row
Swinging around
Up and down

SUN ON THE CLOUD

The sun on a cloud
It looks so pretty to me
I really like it
So do we

CAMPFIRE ON A STICK

Campfire on a stick
Looks so pretty to my eyes

Looks like morning light
The red glows the orange flames
Looks so pretty to my eyes

HAPPY HORRIBLE

I'm so happy I feel horrible
It's like a feeling no one understands
I bet you could not feel it
It's really a big deal

HAPPY FEELING

I feel really happy
I'm all jumpy
I just can't stop
I really need to scream

THE END

Hannah Madison Schultz
Age 7
December 29, 2011
As dictated to Kimann

III. The Losing and the Gaining

YOU SAID

You said
Don't get your hopes too high
You said
Keep to reality
It's not as simple as it seems
It's not as simple as it seems
There's ease in mediocrity
What makes it hard
Is when deep down
You find that what you want
Is more
So much, much more
You want to be the best
Better, for God's sake,
Than you could have ever been before.

You can't believe
The hurt I felt inside
The secret kind that gently cuts
It's not as simple as it seems
The steps you took were not in dance,
You walked out on my dreams.

Could you forsee
The plans I'm forced to make
Could you imagine
How much how little it would take
To bring me to the edge
I've quietly gone beyond the point
That once included you.

I've got to grab the golden ring
Deeply aware of the price it brings
Would one ever have guessed
The joy I would eventually seek
Would be the parting words we speak?

I suppose that's why
Sensible people prefer their easy chairs
They'd rather recline
Than take the dare
Not me
I'll jump
I'll fall
My vision tore down the very walls
That keep you safe inside.
     1991/2011

WHAT YOU SAID

You said what you said
Whether you meant what you said
Back then
Whether you mean it now
What you said is what you said
And those words still hang out in the air
Somewhere
Sadly, they'll always be there
Bumping against the stratosphere
Forlorn bits and pieces
Bouncing off the walls of our collective memory
Burning the rope that spanned the chasm
Of our individuality

I'm glad you said
What you said
What you said
Will make good-bye come that much easier.

Thank God
For the words that come out wrong
Thank God
For the voids where they belong
Thank God
For your easy forgetfulness
Thank God
For the way it put to rest
All the rest
All the rest.

Thank God
For the sleep that separates
Thank God
For the nights that end each day
Thank God
For this march on time
Thank God

For the labels you put on me
Thank God
For how it's now so clear to me
For now I know
It's for the best.

Thank God
For the paths that lead away
Thank God
For the choices that guide my way
I'll thank God
For my eventual peace of mind
I think it's still out there, somewhere

Thank God
For the valiant attempt
That in loss is its own reward
In my heart I know I tried
Yes, I tried,
Oh, how hard I tried.

What you said
What you meant
It's easier now
To say good-bye
So, good-bye
I'm going to be just fine

6-2-92/2011

THE UNSAID

The unsaid
The unspoken
Token forgiveness
Small words, misplaced and broken

The unsaid
The morning bells
The toll uncounted
The souls, mourned in the darkness

The unsaid
The blind reflections
Just empty thinking
Ideas, candy-coated

The unsaid
The angry longing
The touch not fought for
The breath, the cold wind holds it

The unsaid
The unspoken
Token forgiveness
Small words, misplaced and broken

So listen
I hear you
Let me speak too
There are a few words I'd like to say…

3-20-93/2009/2011

FREEDOM I

Your skies have ceilings
Built with boards and nails
Of feelings
Feelings you try not to feel
Stolen dreams
You think you should look the other way
I'm not a thief I want to say
My heart took from you the light of day
The hollow, dutiful dream, once fallowed,
Keeps you safe inside
But I'm gone
I've gone outside
And I'm far away
And I'm outside myself

I am the dew
That shrouds the trees
I am the mist
That clouds the breeze
I could care less
Where I am bound
I've found an ocean within my soul
Inside the pulsing currents flow
Desires I cannot wait to fathom
The possibilities of Me.

1-1992/2010/2011

FREEDOM II

Though your skies had ceilings
Built with boards and nails of feelings
Emotion took me way beyond
I dove headfirst into the blue
I know you'd rather turn aside
Than taste the salt of want
So
Mired in mediocrity
Uniqueness is rhetorical
But
Try me
Test my desires
Outside of you, I'm too alive
I can't ignore it anymore
So let me go
Let me go!
And let me be
Let me be.
You stay safe inside, alright
I'm shooting for the moon.

1-1992/2010/2011

ROUND & ROUND & ROUND

If I'd tried for years
To climb into his heart
If I'd tried for days
To understand his heart
I'd still be speaking in senseless tongues
Ending up where I'd begun
With fruitlessness the only food for thought
I'd be left with to think about
To bring me 'round & 'round & 'round
To end once more where I'd thought I'd start.

I'm drawing pictures in the margins
Where landscapes want to lie
But tear-filled clouds confuse the skies
And contemplation clouds my plight
As I, steadfast, try to intellectualize
The science behind a broken heart.

Sometimes I pretend
I'm steady where I stand
Upon this fragile, new island
Where existence is rendered in quicksand
Sifting shifting, shifting sifting…
I'm dragged down with memories
Of all those crazy should have beens
And with photographs that like bravest soldiers fall
Domino'd smiles, tears and frowns
Fluttering down & down & down & down
That, having flown, gather slow
And melt into the ground.

I'm folding scraps into cheap airplanes
And throwing them away
They trace an awkward question mark
And then collapse and fall apart
As I, steadfast, try to intellectualize
The science behind a broken heart.

There's a circle in my mind
And it goes round & round & round
Its echoes ring with voided circumstance
I hate to hear its sound
There are too many words unsaid
Going round & round & round

All I want now is to still the hurricane
I once named after you.

Round & round & round
The things I never, ever said
Round & round & round & round
The words that never would be read
Round & round & round & round
My thoughts once thrown aside
Round & round & round & round
The letters I will never write
Round & round & round & round
What marks the passing of the tides
Round & round & round & round
Awash within my weary eyes
No sound in silence, no sound, no sound.

4-4-92/2009/2010/2011/2012/2013

AIN'T IT A DAMN SHAME

Ain't it a damn shame
When you finally think it's alright
Ain't it a damn shame
To open yourself up
And here, I'm wasting my damn time
I see myself in puddles on the floor
Scraping my heart up off the boards
Watching me seep beneath the door
Ain't it a damn shame
I should've kept my untried heart
Closed like my eyes against the night
Ain't it a damn shame?

Ain't it a damn shame
I didn't know where I stood
Ain't it a damn shame
I did not understand
In front, behind
Far, far off to the far side
It's a crazy, bent-out shame
I should have let my thoughts go
Like tracking engines in the night
On pre-ordained paths bolted fast
Rushing, rushing, rushing past
Ties that bind
Ties that blind
Ties that only split in time
Splinter, fester then fall off
A falling out
Far too much fallout
Such a waste of time
Of time and too much toil
Too much trouble
It happens every time
Don't it
It happens every time
And when it does

Ain't it a shame
Ain't it a goddam shame

5-12-92/2011/2012

THE BEFORE AND THE AFTER

I think of you
In the before and in the after
Through all your tears
I still hear laughter
'tis a sound that pulls
At the very fiber of my soul
Memories unravel
And forgetfulness is the misshapen shroud
Of lace into which crude messages are woven
That once hid the girlish, little face
Promises and wishful thinking
Once held their token, trifling power
And kept me in my place
The wrappings have now worn out.

My heart has then thought it best
To return into its chest
And there its found its rhythm
Beating, bleating, what's the difference
It resignedly reminds
I am alive,
I am alive
Alive, alive, alive!

All on my own
For no other reason
Than to just Be
Existence requires its own resolve
And so I'll turn from you
As the earth turns slowly from her moon
For one thousand tomorrows beckon
Evenly, yearningly
Farther away
Evolving, evolving,
Revolving, revolving, revolving

3-27-92/2010/2011

NEW HEART

Now I think I can say goodbye
I can see you'll be alright
Neither one of us needs to be
Doing great
Or fabulous, outstandingly, wonderfully,
couldn't be better (but it could)
The stars and flags can wait
Already I can see the worst memories fade
The bad ones likewise dissipate
To stains
Faint on the likewise aging concrete pavers
Annotating an evermore forgotten past.

Not much else left, huh?
The memories I choose to keep
(Small and rare and far too few)
May gain in clarity
Like the wine I now still need for sleep
They will more than last
And they more than suffice
Their small number is merely an affirmation
That this path is now the right one
I have the courage to face the pain
And the strength to cry
I am finally learning
That the falling down
And the allowing for the tears
Are what I need to reach some end
So I can begin again.

Now, I could use a new heart
You see, I think I'd like a fresh start
I've stepped carefully over sparkling shards of pain
And watched my old heart in the rain
Broken, wrapped and tied and stashed
With memories and words unsaid
But guess what?

I've found a someone new
I would like a heart to give him too
For I think that he might be inclined
To keep it with him and intact
And in the future, give it back
But only if I asked
For now, that question I intend to keep to myself
And instead
Ask him more about himself.

5-92/2010/2011

BITTERSWEET

I lost one love
I know I'm not the first to lose
And the trying
Was noble, yes
I found I ended up with less
Empty words no longer blessed
My eyes
They're dry
There's just too much to see
And do each day
And tears, I know, get in the way.

At every turn
I found one more bridge burned
One more promise broken
The heartache
At least reminds
There's something at work deep inside
That beats in spite of foolish pride
I look
At me
And see the question I still keep:
Was it worth it in the end?
Is the bitter worth the sweet?

With every day
I try anew to find my way
Oh, the paths
From which I choose
What insane coaster, riotous mazes
Does one road lead to happiness?
Is one compass letter better than the rest?
I hope I've chosen well
I hope my dream is worth the sleep
Adrift, I wonder what I seek
And so miss
And so long for,

(So tired, I'm oh, so tired)
And that it's there when I'm awake.

Should what's common still make sense
Was my sanity well spent?

Oh, sure, I'll play
I'll tuck my broken heart away
And the reasons
You'll understand
I'll try to read it in your lips
To see beyond your polite eclipse
So forced, so insincere
So not your fault
We're not as tough as I thought we were
Yet
I can't resist the thought of love
Oh, God, I hear the words repeat
Eros' prayer
The song of fools
Hand me thy poisoned stick
My circle in the sand's complete
I'll take the bitter with the sweet
I'll take the bitter with the sweet.

1991/2009/2010/2011

IN THE MIDNIGHT OF YOUR LEAVING

I'd like
To stay
In this shade of twilight tonight
I need the gray
To ease the brighter colors of the day
Images that otherwise neither blur nor fade
Enough to give solace to the eyes
That instead
Slice through each weary lid
And singe the fragments of my mind.

I'll just
Lie back
And rest a while
I'll watch the night
Close in around me
I smile
The dark outside now suits me fine
It fits nicely with
The ragged coat I wear tonight.

These pieces of my heart
Are the splinters I will find
In the cold, cold places deep inside
And in the corners of my mind.
I'll gather myself up in time
To see what's left, what still is mine
And check once more
For subtle signs
I must confess
I wouldn't mind a little happiness.

I'll step back from the world a while
Recede a bit
This tired tide
This profound lack of light
Can hypnotize

Even in its darkness
The error I recognize:
Let others do onto each other
As they would only if for themselves
Why do we hurt each other?
Go for it
So long as I'm not a part of it.

Edges melt
Memories blur and fade
Some disappear altogether
Such memories need not remain
To taunt relentlessly
When enough clouds are already gathered
To usher in cooling tears of rain.

I'd give
Something back
If I could;
If nothing else
Just enough to ease the load
The weight I've long taken from my shoulders
But the void in its wake
Still bends my mind
No psalms
No overt joy
Just one long, long, long sigh.

I dare
Not wish
This wish on anyone
It would not be fair
To force someone to breathe the air
That I, addicted, too long inhaled
What toxic essence is despair
No body needs
To be thus sustained
On such solitary, pithy seeds.

I'd love to turn back the hands of time
Rewrite in Bryonesque rhyme
And find the thief who did the crime
Who stole my heart and ransomed it
Only to have returned it
Shattered, scattered, raped and tattered.

So I dream on, for now
To see beyond, for now
This shade of twilight
Patience, patience,
Wait for the next light!

In the midnight of your leaving
You are gone
And there is nothing left
Nothing
Not
A
Sound.

1991/2009/2010/2011

FACE TO FACE

I want to meet this sadness
Face to face
I don't mind existing for a while
In its perverted state of grace
I kind of feel like wearing black
A fortress or a shroud or something
For that Victorian year or so
Let me acknowledge every doubt
And let me ponder every fear
Then let me watch doubt fall and fold
Into a withered, weathered hold
So I may cast it like a stone
Into a darkened pool
That lake wherein the saddest things
All come home to rest
Into the watery, endless cold
A dark and stunted garden

When I see the surface settle
And I can look back again at me
I'll see
A someone I could stand to live with
Even if in the end alone
And with my gaze interpret anew
An understanding
A wiser means with which to find a smile
And understand the eyes.

1993/2011

LITTLE BITTERS

Invisible hands turn my head
And tell me to look not behind
But ahead
Little bitters make it easier
Misspoken words and misplaced gestures
Bits and pieces of the past
And memories behind have left
An ever fading, waning trail
A wake of tears and sighs
Contemplative, unheard cries…

…and now I feel a little older
the sun's warmth shines a little colder
is this the wisdom I would've fought for?
Do I know more?
I'll take the knowledge,
That little bitter, fallen apple.

1993/2011/2012

DANIEL AND KEVIN

Where did Daddy go?
I wish I could look into your sleepy eyes
And tell you of some noble deed
That called him off
But I can't
I wish I could tell you
He's gone to sea
And that someday he'll be back
But I can't
I wish I could guarantee
His promise of devotion
But I can't
I wish I could promise you
A week of Christmases with him
But I can't
I wish I could tell you
This is who
You should aspire to
But I can't
I wish I could say that
Mommy and Daddy will stay together
And your modern child's fantasy
Of family
Is to be your first reality
But I can't
I wish I could tell you
That it won't hurt
That a bright orange band-aid
Or a kiss
Or a good night's sleep
Would make it better
But I can't
Oh Lord, I can't
I can tell you that I love you
I can tell you that I will always be there for you
I can tell you that I will be tired at times
Too tired to say or do

Whatever it is that I ought to
But in your innocence
And your trust
I will always hope you can somehow understand.

There is a fortune in your smiles
I vow to keep that safe.
This promise is not kept in any file
Or in a house of law
God helped me write it in my own hand
I love you two,
Mommy

5-29-92/2010

DANIEL

Daniel, do you sense
That I'm there at your side
You see too early too clearly
Your little soul strives to understand
Your young heart struggles to comprehend
What lenses were you blessed with
What vision functions as a bitter curse
When all you see
And all you sense
Is over-bright and etched like hardest glass
Your little footsteps falter
For yet, you would rather dance
As a child,
You should have only to play
I want to see you laugh
Smile, sweet
Big-little boy
Please smile for yourself…

…and Kevin tumbles and he jumps
And his little hands like spring-boards plant
Themselves upon an earth that as yet greets him
Blissfully, ignorantly kindly —
It lets him in.
Little piece of cake, this little slice of pie?
KP, my precious life, let's hope.

12-12/31-92/2009/10

WE KNOW

We had a lovely time out west
The trip was all that we had planned
And more
We're sorry to hear about what happened
Surprises like that change so much
For you
Who knew
But we know you'll be alright
You've always been a resourceful person
You have
Really
What you did was probably the right thing
The answers can take a while to find
Some times
We give you credit
We wish you all the best
Take care
Sincerely
Really
Everything is going to be alright

(Now let's get back to our anointed familial perfection)

1-11-94/10-2011

IV. The Incidental & the Awakening

MY OWN TIME

I've had my head held underwater
And I've been told to breathe
In my own time
My own time
I've had my hand pulled in one direction
And the other, in another
It's my own life
Folly or sacrifice
It is mine to live, not yours

Yes, at times I flounder
And, oh, sometimes I stumble
But when it's time for me to breathe
I'll find my bearings and
Draw a better, deeper, longer breath
Than I have ever drawn before

I know they want what's best for me
I know how hard they try
But my mind is mine
The child, the sage yearn yet in tandem
It is still too hard to completely forgive
Harder yet to forget
Though not by choice the slate is smeared
Words' shadows defy obliteration
When memories cling in desperation
On this, I work, I promise

I'll turn this vessel over to the winds
And follow where it takes me
Eyes open, scanning, re-learning
Maths and new equations
So when it's time to see
And when it's time to breathe
I will pull and hold
I'll know when to release
And I will relish the burning in my chest

In
Out
In
Out

12-12-92/2011/2012/2-16-2013

BREATHE   (My Own Time II)

I took a journey,
Once,
On a long ago and far away
I leapt in through the windows
Of a soul I wished to fathom
Sharks with their needled smiles in hiding
I accepted
A diadem of tears and pearls
(innocent vanity), I wore it
Of briny, shadowed hues
I drank deeply
Recklessly, thirstily
Though the wine
Its heady ribbon,
Its sensuous webbing
Tangled, painful, tear-wrenching
Ensnared as surely as the rarest web of gold
And lo, I am the solitary creature
Dressed in such, no where to go
Left merely looking for my lowly mate
Beyond the reaches of
The everyman's sun
We needed no words

I've had my head
Held underwater
And I've been told to breathe
In my own time
In my own time
I'll find you in the deep, dark side
And take you deep inside
There is a deeper breath
To be drawn
Than I have ever gasped before
In, in, in, in....

1991/2010/2011/2012/2-16-2013

UNTASTED

Untasted
You are the might have been
That wasn't
What could have come
To be
Did not

Untasted
Your chalice is nothing more
An empty cup
I sampled the dream
Risked the burn
Refracted through my translucent shield

I saw a story
With you in it
But when I looked
Nothing was intended
All I could do
Was brush against you
And talk politely of the weather

Untasted
I'll just go on
Smoothed down edges
Thank you Time
My desire
The days will paint
In colors ever cooler
The flame-whipped patterns
Book-marked, no longer read
Some twisted in a tangled ever after
You are
After all this time
Untasted
And so you will remain.
Fade.

7-22-01/2009/10/2011

IN THE GALLERY

In among this galaxy of souls
We are lonely hearts
Innocently seeking highly contrived and carefully orchestrated
chance encounters
Hoping that just one, small aspect might fit
With our own jagged and scarred raw edge

In the gallery
Where flesh and fruit are one
We stepped back from a painting
Let out eyes blend the
Textured streaks
Intellectualizing
Musing as if it mattered
I explained the finer points
Of Seurat's technique
And all I want
Is to touch your skin
There,
Where the collar ends.
I explained
And you listened
You nodded
As if you wanted to comprehend
When all you want
Is to take my earring in your teeth

We moved on to a triptych
Studied it closely
As if we needed to see
Some infinitely important, historically meritorious, sublimely
executed detail
Reveling in each other's auras,
Which had already begun to merge

1991/2009/10/2011

WHO ARE YOU?

I fear your touch
I am afraid that I might like it
Way too much
Don't look like that into my eyes
The question in your gaze
Reaches far too deep inside
The words you speak
God, what a song, they soothe
My soul
Recognizes the dreams you have
What is the force that drives you?
I am afraid of what I feel
It feels too wonderful
My senses reel
I'm trying hard
Not to let myself go
To be too honest with myself
To acknowledge
The crazy I could be about you

Please, let us not speak
That one, little heart-bound word
Keep me in an illusion
Of all that seems
As seen in perfect, momentary present tense
You inspire me
You intrigue me
Your flaws might yet endear me
Who
Are
You?
1991/2009/10/2011

SAVE ME

I want to see you again
Where passion is life
And your kisses are ripe
With the seething
Of hot and whispered, blended breathing
As we gasp
And halfway hope
That no one else can hear
But yet, oh,
If they could see
The perfect, primitive, potent weave
Of intertwined arms and limbs
As energies and selves are spent
And where it is my sanity went
I no longer know
Nor longer seek.
Come,
Trace a path along my cheek
And southwards
To uncertain, certain pleasures
Coupled within the simple, salty pressure
'tis a feast
We dine tonight
Hedonists, biologically submissive
Mixing our respective memories
So that the aftertaste
Has a one and familiar flavor

You called yourself my dream
Did you know
That I'm your angel and you cry,
"Save me!"
I will show you heaven
whenever, wherever

1991/2010/2011

APERETIF

You are
The first drink
Of an amber sherry
I've kept cool and dark
Through the heated months
Now the taste
Slips down my throat
And warms me to my very soul
It settles in a pool beneath
The cool, indiff'rent self I preach
I am incredibly hot for you
I am indelibly marked by you

I drink one glass
Can't quite see straight
I want another, anyway
The thought of you
The way you taste
Creates a rhythmic, awkward gait
No longer one for tasks
Or walking
No longer one for cultured talking
It is a driving,
Sensuous beat
That kindles only one kind of heat
A heat for you
A need for you
Share ye, share me
Warm us through
And through
And through
And through

1991/2010/2011

APPETITE

Cool air caresses me
Underneath those woolen folds
All I wear
Is the heart I've bared
For you
In spite of having lived so very long
So fed up
For far too long
One thing I've learned anew
Is that
I am starved
Now starved for you
I don't give a damn
I have this,
This desire
It devours me
Though I eat and eat and eat
I am okay with the utter absence of a need to quit
Not interested in being satiated

A ribald poignancy,
A lusty poet's sensuous prose
Have I said too much?
I want to say much more
What I will do
To all of you
Will turn their heads
I know how I've turned yours.

1991/2010/2011

BACK TO YOU

See me
In a shadow of winter white
Greet me
With your soft, enfolding touch
Wrap me in you
Hold me tight
Put away
Reality
Fold away
The masks and smiles we wear
Tear at me
'til I'm defenseless
Let me go
Then see me
Coming back to you

1991/2011

I AM STRONG ENOUGH TO CATCH YOU

I'm too naïve
In love, oh love,
I'm innocent
Though I've been through so much
I've got a long, long way to go
Your lessons have taught me well
I was fourteen again in your car
I was sixteen again in your bed
And you, my sad and sweet young man,
You are only twenty-two
Going on forty-two
What hand has lady life dealt you
Why is your perfectly, correctly
Executed demeanor
Barely hiding the bitterness beneath?
I thought my heart could stoke
Your soul,
I thought I could affect that dry-iced wit
Imbue you with a bit of warmth
But your heart is packed away
'neath your cool and ever-present sphere
Of self-serving calculation.
Falter
Just once,
Break your own, self-imposed rules
And call me
I am strong enough to catch you.
If you'd let yourself stumble
Like we humans are wont to do
I could help you back up again too
And still keep a fair amount of the hard-won illusion intact
That you, damn it,
Still hold for me

1991/2010/2011/2012

I CAN WAIT

Do you
Do you want me
Do you
Do you want me to be
Do you
Do you want through me to be
The who
The who you'd always hoped to be?

By me
On my same side
By me
By my same side day and night
By me
By my side 'til morning light
Your eyes
Should be there to greet mine.

It's alright
I can wait
Someday we'll be together
I can wait
I can wait
Someday we'll be together
I can wait
I can wait
Someday we'll be together…

2-1-92/2011

FOREVER IS ALLOWED

Twisted words and meanings
Tangled thoughts, misguided dreamings
There's a web of wording out there
A constellation yet unfound
Ungrounded in a fantasy
That forever's not allowed…

Forever is allowed
In war it's honor bound
In love 'tis what I found
So won't you feel it too
Won't you feel it like I do?

You've built yourself up so well
So self-contained, intellectual
Why do I sense a hint of fear
When you talk about yourself
That you want to stay forever free
To want someone is greed?

Are soldiers dominos
Lined up to watch each other fall
Chain reaction, misintention
Misguided, devotion-rich religionized
One by one they all fall down
And forever rest alone…

If tinsel trickles make-believe
Silver for the common man
Runs like water through the hand
No fanfare nor applause
Or words composed and color-matched
Can catch hold of each little breeze
And lighten up
All our dark thoughts

Be they ever green

7-27-92/2011

STREET OF DREAMS

Hey cab man
You there
Flag me down an ordinary conveyance
Take me gone
No, not home
I'm still stumbling along a street of dreams
I have no idea where to
Hey woman
Lookin'
Tempt me with a glance, a smile
Easily won
Too readily down
This muddling, beaten path beats me
The street of dreams leads nowhere

Hey mama
I know
I never understood
You tried
If in quiet moments a furtive sigh
The pointlessness belied
The fact that most ships never arrive
Hey baby
Small human
Who dared clip off your wings?
Fledgling person
Neon lamb
Your ship is still at hand

Hey brother
Walkin'
Do you want to ride
I won't lie to you, my momentary friend
Or treat you wrong
Take to this street of dreams with me

Hey mirror

Musin'
Please don't laugh when you look back at me
Pyrite paved for all fools' sakes
The only real obstacle is fear
No, stay clear
Reflect a better me
Show me a different street of dreams
Before the locomotive hits

10-15-92/2009/2010/2011/2012

1992

1992
Fresh and fruitless
Oh, 1992
A year gone by
So self-indulged
The thin one's fed
The blond one's put her clothes back on

1992
What crooked cross hangs
By your front door
When east went west
And the sun went down
Fear kept her in her midnight
Oh, 1992

1992
Home again, but no one's there
Mommy, daddy's in the sun
They locked up all their little ones
Some happy Happy Hour that is
So, Hollywood, are you the one who taught us?

1992
Oh, Lord,
The president can play the blues
Southern comfort in his tunes
The wisemen on the Hill seem soothed
For, better times are ahead
Better time's ahead
Oh, 1992

1992
At least, at last
I think we're through
I'm working on 2000
And hoping there is something left

For my sons and for your daughters
1992

1992
Hold out your hands
And let me put in them a little sand
Let's see how quickly it falls on through
December's kicking, midnight calls
Let's put away another day
And call this one a year.
   12-21-92/1-6-93/2009

CLOSE IN THE DISTANCE

If I need to
I'll keep my distance
But I don't want to
I like the idea of having you
I like the way you move
I like the way you sound
I like to hear what you have to say
I find myself
Closing in on you
Leaning, listening
I am thinking
I want the only distance between us to be
The moments between our kisses

Closing in the distance
Between our kisses
Close to the instant
Where one kiss ends
And the next kiss has begun
Yes

I can be polite
To hell with etiquette
I want to chase you down
Past the mundane everyday
I want to corner you with my desire
The steam our breath makes
Between each give and take
Should be all that marks
The pauses between our kisses

Open your eyes wide
Open up your mind
There's so much to be learned
Ignorance, my sweet, holds no bliss
Nor should it hold back you
Convention's tossed into the winds

Foundations free-formed, built to last
By artists
Builders
Lovers' craft
Call it what you will
I'll walk with you through galleries
I'll see you and you'll see me
On half-shell beds we'll stand apart
From the draped, offended masses
Fuck off, you tranquil seas

I'll keep my distance
But it won't be easy
My need is my disease
Your invitation, your welcoming words, the timbre in your voice
Come now
Come take a chance
Let questions mark
The needs we both possess
Move heaven and earth with me, my sweet
Close the distance between our kisses

I want you to pretend no more
That you don't want me any less
Than I with all my being want you
Nearer
Nearer
Nearer still
Come, close in the distance

5-1-92/2011/2012

DISTRACTION

This morning I gotta think it over twice
Which way is left
Which way was right
I never, ever realized
That heaven could be so close by
I see your voice
I hear you looking down to me
I feel your sigh wafting through me
Oh, what a distraction
There is no question
Nor satisfaction
Until I see you again tonight.

Sidewalks alive with the human sea
Buildings bend
Say, 'hi' to me
Laughter hides beneath the sun
Magic stirs like cream in my coffee
The way you touched me
The way your kisses talked to me
The way your eyes reflected back to me
A me I truly relished
What I learned last night
Answered so many questions
Bereft by day of satisfaction
I need to hold you again tonight.

I like the geometry
Of fine design and lines and curves
Pulsing pieces I crave like food
Your smile invites me to your table
Your body is my banquet
Satiate me

My computer possesses a sexier voice
My cluttered desk has room for you
Clothing falls to the floor like leaves

Human flaws precious, incidental
Chemically perfected
The image I hold will hold me through
Until my ordinary day is done
And I am on my way back home
The highway that is time and legitimate obligation
Unwinds its length to make way for you

Good intention is to find what pleases
To find what steals the breath away
To find the story's sweet conclusion
That in a whispered sigh pleads "Stay"
And keeps you in my bed
So that after all has been said and done
I at last can drift off to dark in the circle that is you

5-1-92/2011

YOU GOT ME

You are a benchmark, baby
A craftsman's credit is
Second to none
Anthems, baby
Songs to love
We came together
Came undone
You raised my colors, baby
My flag is flying
In your name
My standard's getting higher
You're pulling on my reigns
You got me
You got me
Is love a game, a type of war
When lust throws caution
To the winds
And the sky has lost its limit
Leave my resolve in tatters, baby
I'm crawling on your ground
Horizons delineated by
Your smiles and arms and legs 'round mine
The planetary edge reached only by desire
You got me
You got me
Your eyes can find me in the dark
Your talons will soon find their mark
Surrender lies within my heart
What brought us together
What tears asunder
Collapsed and fell
We fall apart
You got me
You got me

3 & 7-93/2011

EVER SINCE

Our paths have crossed
Just once or twice
I know you've seen me watching you
I know you've watched me too
Could you have guessed my wondering
What thoughts I will have kept
To my silent, smiling, suffering self
But want, I know, like sunlight shows
On the day my heart first leapt
The day I first saw you

Some night I promise
I will come
On dreams' soft and silent wing
I will slowly, sleepily seduce
The helpless, slumbering you
I will be everything
You could ever dream to dream about
What secrets love can bring
Before the morning violently slings
My veil down to the floor
And I am forced to leave

I promise to have touched you with my soul
You will have longed for me
You will evoke the vague memory
With a nameless, nostalgic ache
Though you as yet don't know me

1991/92/2011

IN A WAKE

Simplicity deceives
Soft deception's mask we wear
Illusions of the storms we bear
What's true reality?
Who's right?
Who's wrong?
Which one of us needs to move on?
I am awake
In her wake
I exist in the giving and the taking
Our time apart is irrelevant
I the child have chosen to believe
That what we share is worth the fallout
When I close my eyes
She is there
Peeking sadly through the portal
I take the unguarded exit
My dignity requires it
My conviction for us protects it
When we open all and pass beneath
One day for all the world to know
We'll ask Time for immunity
We'll ask the Fates for their blessing

When the circle finds you I will be there
When the circle breaks I will be there
When the circle drowns I will be there
I close my eyes and you will be there
I open my heart and I'll find you there

3 &18-92/2011 KA w/ MLS

WATERCOLOR WORDS

There's a waterfall
In what you have just said

The words you spoke
Took the words that I once wrote
And washed them off the page

What I thought would be our history
Is and will not ever be

You are fading
You are more transparent
Than you were a year ago
You are fading
I can put my hand right through your image echo
Doesn't honesty
Sometimes take a colorful, shadowed rendition
And turn it into a washed-out notion
That like a spill furtively slips off the fresh-stained page

What I thought would be our history
Is and will no longer be
You are fading
Ever more
And we will be
Nevermore
From this and all days forward

5-3-92/2009/2011/2012

V. The Redefining of Love

HERE I AM

Here I am
A thinking fool who thought I knew
What love was all about
What I know now
Transforms the texts
Dissolves the illuminated manuscripts
To something colored between the lines
But I wouldn't change a thing
The contrast helps me to see
What love can and should not be

There I was
In innocence rather desparate
Did I grasp with all I had back then
What greed ever did anyone good?
What desire ever drove anyone closer
Only to yank so far away
The lives created within that world
These are with me still
Nearly grown, angelic dregs
From erstwhile clouds have flown

There I was
When I first understood
What had at first been solitude
Was instead a loneliness
Quiet and cold
So upon one winter's lonely eve
I burned the photographs
And hid away the ashes
Saw answers intermingled with the shadows
Youth's dimly lit resolve
Gave way to fledgling maturity
You soon enough peered around the corner
Music was to be found, already in the stars

Here I am

And still amazed
At all the people around me
Enveloped in their vapid mediocrity
While you are now so close to me
And with me fight off the ordinary
And drab reality
The calm contains the colors
So wonderfully
And quietly
Leaves me to still believe
There's still room for the dreaming

Here we are
Here we can be
Whenever and where ever
Our small eternity.

10-30-01/2009/2011

I DO

...because we're friends, we share
and care as humans tend to care
we build pathways day after day after day
and burn as many bridges along the way
sometimes the words we try to say
are caught in the webs of day to day
I catch myself still longing for all
I never got to do

Who has a simple life
Who wants to redefine
Who really ever needs no one
Who wants to just belong?
I do!
I do!

1992/2-19-2013

THE REDEFINING OF LOVE

26 x 25 x 24 and on to one
When all of a sudden
One
Makes a little less sense
And we begin to realize
Why She was made to
Walk garden paths
Already complete in themselves

She held her,
Bewildered
Thankful yet frightened
And unfulfilled
Some run and so she did
Now She in turn
Has learned to hold
As well,
And begins to understand
Because a bond is there,
Which exists far beyond
Convention and tradition
Cradled against the untouched, puritanical breast
An imperfect bed
Desired, all the same

What simple, immaculate architecture
We are the diminutive reflections
Of all temples
Huts, shacks, tract houses
Our cathedrals
Rise with spires never static,
Our foundations are never the tomb

We who love best
Are asked to give up
What we love best
If we could more fully understand

We would rejoice in sublime loss

1992/2010/2011

CHRYSALIS

Rooms have doors for reasons
They sometimes answer
Questions composed in sleep
Yet fear
For all the right reasons
Exists
Allow at least a window
To see beyond the obvious
And a mirror
To see whatever self looks back
In time,
The time you choose
Will find you and find you ready
So choose it well
I will be there to greet you.

There is so much to you
Waiting
Impatient, wishful emergence
Too much to hold back
To let lie
Let go of
Though I cannot be the one
To frame the door
Or unlock it
Or to rearrange the room
The house inside your heart
Should be the only one that counts
I will be there to greet you

I shall be a part of that next residence
I will probably
Lay claim to a room or two alongside you
We have already shared so much
And there's so much more to do
There are no limits
No ceiling slapped above us

No blinds to block the light
Promise to remember that
Happy Birthday, Michael.
I could say more
But I won't
I fear myself a little
What words might write them selves
Having taken wing
So I won't

1-26-92/2010/2011

THAT LINE

Where have you been
All these lonesome years
Who's held you
Kissed your breath away
Who dried your tears
Who lay with you
What choices did you make
That led you now my way
Now that we're here
Don't be afraid
Don't be in awe of me
I'm only me
And if I happen to be the one
You've been searching for
So what
I've been searching for you, too.
So, go ahead,
Look deep and long
Into my eyes
I have nothing at all I need to hide
May you see everything
You want to see
Hope to see
Need to see
Until the only think lacking
'midst the gaze as we both hold it
is the touch
of my lips
upon yours.

1-28/29-92/2010/2011

THE LANDSCAPE OF YOUR LOVE

Now that the harbor of your trust
Is mine
The valley of you arms
Is why
I'm a shepherd bringing in
My forlorn flock of fears
I want to lay them down to rest
And put them all behind me
Leave for me a scrap of paper
With a few lines laid down in red
It's the only map I need
To see the landscape of your love

I wondered then
Am wandering still
The treasure tucked within your breast
Is worth a life's long journey
The hills
The falls
Translucent walls
I'll bravely take them on
A journeyman in love and longing
Hungry with desire
Thirsty for the spring
Willing
So willing
To give so much to you
Freely
So freely
I am your pennies from heaven
I am the soil beneath your step
I am the stars you see at night
I am the essence of your sleep
Just how much,
How in my love I could be for you.

1991/2010/2011

YOU ASK

So you ask
So I will tell
I'll speak softly
Won't break the spell
Do I love you?
It's not a question
Anymore
How could I love you
Even more?
When do I think of you?
Do I think of you? I think of you
At night
I think of you
In the morning
I think of you
In the after
I think of you
In the before
I think of you
So deep inside
My mind will keep you
Hold you tight
For ever, ever more

So dear
Draw near
Don't speak another word
We are long past ordinary lovers' questions

May the world turn on in silence
Upon its silver axis
We'll turn with it, upon it
A warm spot on its face

1991/2009/2010/2011

HEALING KISSES

I came to you
A whole person
Because I like who I am
I came to you
Hurting
Because I am human
Because I had been looking
In all the wrong places
For love
For some naïve notion of eternity
In 2 months
You've loved me 10 years' worth
Your kisses
Suit my new found lack of pain
They smooth
The roughest grain
And edge me past
Anything I had ever expected
Without the healing kiss of you.

1992/2009/2010/2011

I'M SORRY

I'm sorry for the way I felt
I'm sorry for the things I said
But until reality catches up
With our dreams
Those songs are all I have.
Today the pain is as real
As my love for you is ethereal

3-22-92

JOY

We are roads
That lead in circles
Back to ourselves
We are hills
Ridges, valleys, fields
We are natives
Savage, innocent
And pilgrims
Blind, stunted, well-intended
Finding worth in each new season
Sowing
Hoping
When love takes root
Questions
Doubts
Remembrances of the future
Lying wide awake at night
And listening
To the
Gentle rolling, stretching as the
Full moon rises low and
Presents its sun-bent face
Full upon ours
I throw myself over the edge
My falling is now beyond me
Your eyes hold me
As only eyes can hold anyone
Free falling
Falling
Life
Cries.

2-13-92/2009/2010/2012

CLOSE TO FAR AWAY

I
Mama
We're close to far away
Aren't we, Mama?
We're close to far away
My love
So close to far away
So, close your eyes
My little one
There's little else to say
Reach between the day
Where dreams tease as if reality
And darkness is the blanket pulled
Over lucid feelings
Where and when you see me
Pretend that I'm not there
I am the love that is everywhere
And you have all lords and gods behind you
So long as I command it
Be autonomously one and whole
So close to far away
Reach between the dream and day
So close is far away
So close,
So far away…

II
My love
You're close but far away
Whey then, love?
Do you understand my love
What words
Describe emotions,
These…these…
Feelings,
They weaken me
They've taken everything from me

Reach between my hands
And find the heart enframed
Where blood thickens
Lust quickens
Love in the rough
What diamond lies unearthed!
A fledgling spirit, work undone
From within a sky that holds little welcome
The curve of our small earth
Is all the horizon we need to conquer
Simple knight, save me

Endless,
Sleepless…sleepless…
Reach between my hands
And take the heart enframed
Consider me as one alone
Whole without you but better still
When there, right there, beside you
There to follow
There to guide you
You're close, but far away
As I am too
Let me destroy your constellation
And claim your light as mine.

11-30-92/2009/2010/2011

MY WALK

I started my walk
Through the forest dark
And turned a new leaf
To see the green beneath
I found a younger prince
Who with a fresh, new breath
And energized in love
Soft shadowed me from above
And held me in security below
(Will he ever let me fall?)
When thoughts soar impossibly
And faith her head holds loftily
Youth catches up
With wisdom
That burns through innocent's might
The morning comes
And I see the lines
And like them
And I will cross them
I will always love you
Let us take this world on
And touch between times
I will always
As friend
Be there for you
I hope always
As love
To be there too.

11-19-92/2009/2010

YOUR VOICE YOUR SONG

You won't need to bring me roses
I like the flowers in the field
I don't need diamonds and pearls
The earth rests quiet beneath
And the sea can keep her secrets.
Sing from your heart
It's a caress that begins
At the crest of my being
And slowly washes over me
Until I am wrapped in only
The electric warmth of your song
And the sound of your voice
Which, breathed into me, gives to my soul new flight.

It was not
Just coincidence
Was it
That I mentioned
A piano and a player
Then a
Church and a prayer
In the same breath
And it was not
Was it
Just a coincidence
That you said
You had written those very words
A few, short light-years ago
Was it
Was it?

No.

1-28-92/ 2009/ 2010

WAITING WAITING

It's the same snow
On the ground
That fell last night
With you inside
All I can do is wait tonight
I cannot call
For someone else might answer the phone
Oh, God,
I know you want to be with me
As much as I want to be with you
But in this dream of love and lust
Will the impossible eventually come true?

Somewhere beyond
Our everyday
You've touched me deep inside
And now I find I'm wanting
You right here
Right by my side
Oh, you can feel
The words I think
With you I am so very whole
Without I'm torn apart.

So call me
Call me
Come to me
Defy the night
Reality
Will be within our warm embrace
The light of love illuminates
The very stars
Which matter not
The sun
Matters even less
The moon is mine for a song
When I'm with you

There are fortunes in your gaze
And paradise is a place
My everyday calls home.

2-10-92/2009/2010

I'M HERE

Picturing you in my heart and mind
Knowing that our thoughts still touch
Wondering what you're saying now
Feeling this sweet and gentle half-lifed crush

In what I do or where I am
I'll never be alone again
Though others take your strength and time
Doubt and shadows die:
You're mine

I know your heart is mine
I've never been this sure of anything before
What this dark and dreamy destiny
Holds captive for us two
I do not know
I'm not so sure
All I know is that a part of me
Is trav'lling at your side
I've come along just for the ride
Just beyond your waking sight
Whisp'ring through the dreams you make
To touch you in the night
And hold you to the blinding light
I'm here

Billboards mark the endless miles
You read me into every word
How did I fall inside your hands
Breathing in the air you breathed?

How is it that the night we had
Seems now so distant, lost and vague
Convince our minds to hear our hearts
And hope to change what keeps apart

Although this room is still

The silent echoes here will never sound the same
Although you're light years distant from me now
The same moon taps at your window
Your heart is here, as mine is there
And though all the claim I have to you
Is what our hearts suggest
Shivering, stripped of all pretense
I ask you to
Anticipate me, love
Come back to me, my love
I'm here.
I'm home.
Open up the doors
I'm there as much as you are here
And more
Oh, so much more
I'll never have enough
Tonight I'm left with less
Years of miles lie between
Your heart and mind and what I breathe
In and out
The air you gasp
Think harder still
Bring it to an anguished rasp
I will from here ignite the nerves
That crest your soul
And write the words
You'll want to hear
Each time you come back for more
I am here
I am here.

2-21-92/2009/ 2010/2-19-2013

THE FIRST OF LOVE
I
We're conditioned
To live in compromise
So what we want
Is less and less
When all of a sudden,
Less is suddenly not enough
The edge of life becomes less rough
I guess I could get used to you
And to this happiness.

Who are you
To take my world
And turn it 'round
To take all that
I thought I had
And turn it upside down
What is this thing
You've given me
It's craziness
But all of it makes so much sense
I feel your soul
All over me
Why do I feel
So very free?
Is this the first of love?

What was it
In a song that moved
And knew me inside out
What did you say
That others had already said
But, oh, so diff'rently
To somehow strike me to the core
And gently break the lock
I'd long since stashed
Long thought safe and cool
Is this the first of love?

II
I'd been conditioned
To accept compromise
So what I saw
Was colorless
Those shades are suddenly not enough
My light in life is no mirage
I guess I could get used to you
And to this happiness.

Why have I
So long without
Lived in a world I believed my lot
And thought what was
My everyday
To be the only one
Alone's one thing
I could live with
Involuntary solitude
But loneliness
Existed in a line so fine
There to be
Overstepped and tripped by it all
I want to fall
Into your arms
Is this the first of love?

III
There are conditions
I need to emphasize
For what I want must always be
No more or less than what you would want of you
What I would want of me
Our slice of life should cut an edge
And over time stay bright and fresh
Swing wide the door for both of us
Jointly and as sole proprietor of self
And you, now you

And now this happiness.

IV
I see a vision
As pure as winter white
Of promises
Unspoken words
That hold their own beneath any heavy sky
Once we step beyond the ledge
And feel the wind rush by
We fall
Held by our happiness.

V
…and yet I fear
To lose this fear
Sweet fear, this first of love.

2-1-92/ 2010/2011/2-19-2013

MARKING TIME

On a Sunday morning
All is as it should be
The sunlight dances in the trees
The birds sing from behind the leaves
The coffee tastes good, warm and fresh
But the simple order of my world
Is slightly out of line
Your face was not there
Smiling from across the bed
There was just a vacant pillow
To greet me in your stead
I'm only marking time…

Until I'm free to call you mine
I'm only marking time
One, two, three, four, five…

In a single lifetime
We tally up the days
The happiness we hold inside
Pain we try to take in stride
The love we learn to love holds true
But these feelings paint a darker hue
You image dances on that shadowed plane
Everything I touch
Touches me back and feels like you
You can't be here tonight
To make this momentary wrong seem right
I keep on marking time…

In an age-old chapel
Hand-painted on the walls
The martyred figures still hold court
What suffering was their reward?
Displace passions, lover-marked
Parched and painted faces peel
And fall like unintended mosaics to the streets

My portrait could be up there
Who needs such unforgiving bookmarks?
My religion is my love
I pray
Sending unholy thoughts your way
In the manner of my pious kin
And still I'm marking time…

Set yourself up to the skies
Kiss me with your breath of life
And start your life with me
Come, start your life with me
Look at me with freedom's eyes
Come, start you life with me

3-22-92/2011/2-19-2013

PLAY ME

It's not just that you love me
It's the way you love me that I love
It's not just that you talk to me
It's the words and how you say them
It's not just how you look at me
It's how I can look at you
I am everything
I am yours
I am all instruments you have learned to play
I am yours in every way
Such beauty borne of a simple girl
Now I am your woman
You make me ageless
With a love that is timeless
You are mine
Oh, yes,
And I am yours.

3-16-92/2011

TERMS

I became the wanderer
With this pack against my back
Within it is a decade of life, all wrapped and tied
My staff still seeks the fountains
I love the plains and sometimes still fear the mountains
My coat of virgin wool long turned
Into the finest suit of mail
Each link was forged with love and hate
I learned to wear it rather well
Calloused shoulders, arms and legs
And now you're here, undo me
And now you're here, you've moved me
As we've walked into this love
This love, this song that's taken on a life all of its own
My terms are simple,
They are merely this:
I come into this just as I am
I will be the me I've found
That somehow always was so simply me
You be the one who you were so wonderfully anyway
That way, in all of our togetherness
We can still be free
I came into this thing of ours a trifle jaded
A little torn
This soldier's heart has seen the miles
And searched too far and way too long
The memories and enemies of too much time
Apparent and defaulted
Hang and cling
Evil monkeys, albatrosses
You ask if you can help to pull them off
And with them take my guard
Well, lay them down
Let the burden slowly go
It hurts and it is tender still
I am certain the scars will show
But if you speak the best of words

The vines and traps will fall
Like the slightly sad and wasted effort of my long agos
Call my name
Just loud enough
Soft words can cut
So use their edge to pry my heart
That is the way
I want these things to be
For that is how what we believe we want
Can last
And I want as us
Our lives to pass.

4-24-92/2011/2012

IS THERE?

Is there a baby
Out there somewhere
Yet to fall softly into my arms and his
I've never caught a falling star
But many a wish
I have placed
Many a dream
Has caught my gaze
May the dream for once catch me

What you do to me
What you do to me
Oh, Lord, what you do to me

Now that I know you
I can't have known you soon enough
I wish I'd known you yesterday
And all my yesteryears

I'm no rash risk taker
But for you I'd take the dive
I'm merely mortal
But for you I'd stay alive
And leave the dying
To their despair

3-1992/2011

A MAN, TWO BOYS

There's nostalgia in the first real snows
My child feels the promise of the laughter and the holiday
My woman sees you coming up the walkway
Such a promise of love
The wonder of it all

I'm a part of this shook-up world
A piece of all this craziness is yet a sweet reality
The snow brings home the power of a memory
The kiss was an elixir
A touch that sent me soaring

And you're eight hours away for just another day
And I'm dealing with the joy and trepidation
Only once-broken hearts ever recognize
And, oh, Lord, I miss my boys

12-23-93

EXODUS/GENESIS

Is Exodus the same as Genesis
When I ask my son, would he like to go West
And I see his eyes could stand more big-country skies
And I forage over grassy fields to grasp a small group of hands
And I crawl over deserts to reach their sweet souls
Is Exodus the same as Genesis
When starting over means closing up shop
Too long I've played the curator
Taking care of a decade of memories and mementos
(Small trinkets they've become)
Prone to dust and casting shadows
I wish to clear out at long last
I'm no clinger to the past
(Though I do not want to forget)
I want to play the pioneer
Perhaps the bohemian
I want to try again
I want to learn to play
The words are fuzzy
The step is vague
There's a dance in all this somewhere
And a bundle of years ready to shrug off
There are two shoulders that wish to
Draw two arms up toward the sky
And re-learn to fly.

6-2-93/2011/2012/2-19-2013

THE PLACE OF ALL SENSES

...to lose yourself in a place
emotion-carried in a maze
the place of all senses
where reason, intuition bend
and chaos paints in colors blended
pinwheel-circuits running red
like torrents crashing in your head
as memory and future fuse
into a perfect, momentary present tense
and tension builds
and then explodes
yes, passion has a heavy hold
and curiosity's sensual whisper blows
through your hair and through your soul
there's nowhere else you want to be
all else
could not be less relevant
in the place
of all senses
in the place of all senses

1-2-95/10-2011

LIFE IMITATES ART

All that I am sure of
Is that nothing is for certain
Throw back the curtain
And let the show begin

10-94

BREATHE ME

To inhale a bit of your soul
To go where you don't let
Too many people go
An island
An addict's sanctuary
A kiss that could be
Eternity
Never ending
Breathe me, says he
Oh, baby, breathe me

To transfix upon your face
To look behind that sweet façade
To feel what's there
The labyrinth that you are
This is a mystery in which
Lost I want to be
Groping harder
Finding secrets
And drunk upon them

It's a kiss that could be
Never ending
Eternity
Breathe you
Breathe me
Breathe in and out your soul
Caress the spirit
Caress the moment
I want to be the ashen X on your forehead
Breathe you
Breathe me, says he
Breathe me

11-8-94/1-8-95/10-2011

VI. Rugs on Puddles/Coats Over Oceans

OUR LADY

The echo like a marionette
Hangs from midnighted corners
The fretwork forms a skeleton of stone
Pipes of brass and hollow cane
Somewhere, within all that, the seraph came
It's as much the chords you played
As what you did not say

In the face of her kaleidoscope
The shards of beauty's spectrum
Which wavelength takes you closer to heaven's crest?
Ecstasy and innocence
Absorbed, adrift in frankincense
It's as much on her you preyed
As those you yet forsake

Hidden in a box of gilded truths
The proof remains a thing of secrets
Mysteries and miracles pull at the clasp
The scalloped edges of their wings
Betray, deny the Everyday
It's as much the rules you make
As what your Fathers tell you to break

So, the rock of all islands
Perches
Uneasy as a dove
Impaled with signals from above
Tuned in to fatally flawed humanistic frequency
Elevation is but a simpleton's notion of devotion
Deified sanctified
Dogmatically insured

My lady
Rest your soul
Your beauty serves you well
For, though the scripted cuts cannot be read

They want so badly to believe
They so want to belong
You want them at any cost
You got them but at what price
A coin, a heart, a well-trained mind
Art for the ages, art to bribe
Ashes set adrift
By winds of any mean and merchant choice
And for them
To rise
In time
To you
What is the no-man's truth?

4-10-92/2009/2-20-2013

YOUR NAME

You're ice cold to the touch
But if you could
I'd bet you'd reach out and touch me too
You'd reach through your thick haze of frost
Through countless, ageless, time-drenched years
You'd cry a single, solemn tear
If only that you would
Your frozen heart forgot the tune
And words, pre-crafted, still elude
If drumbeats marked your hard-won life
Their echoes did not hold long enough

Look out from 'neath your half-closed eyes
If you could only see
Would sight curse you with
A new-found overwhelming fear
For what little you knew, you knew well too
And though small by contrast
It was your paltry, honest all
The students now just want to know
What your dregs can here impart
From mountain fields that fed your flock
To mold-encrusted sentiments
Cast footprints filled with sediment
What is there to decipher?

Take the cave Madonna's outstretched hand
Escape the howling winds that threaten
Tell her you love her
Even if a half-baked ruse
A primitive desert served up for two
But hurry though
Before the blizzard gets much worse
You may never see her face again

We see that worry maps your brow
We muse on pain you could have been spared

As life was taken by degrees
And your cries were called in vain
What with a hunter's meager meal
Petrified in what was once your core
(If only of this simplest of pleasures you could once more partake!)
What with a primitive bed for sleep
Perhaps a fresh hewn woman for your dreams
No; 'twas but a humble shepherd's wish for safety
For himself and for his lowly sheep

Take the unkempt child's outstretched hand
Teach her all you once had learned
Show her how to lay the stones
In rows for imbeciles to read
All manner of drama, joy, and sorrow
Decipherable for now, only to you
Don't you wish you could give them count
You could have conceived for us a calendar
So we could better count now on you

Take therefore the hand we extend
Great minds can make the best of friends
Know your dignity will be somewhat spared
For we cannot help but ask: Were you are you well endowed?
Go ahead and tell us more about yourself
You are for now a celeb, a star
But however much you might teach us
However unwillingly that might be done
In the end there's one question left
We still won't know your name.

3-16-92/2009/2011/2012/2-20-2013/12-19-2024

Requiem for the Alpine Ice Man, discovered September 1991

RUGS ON PUDDLES/COATS OVER OCEANS

Rugs on puddles
Coats over oceans
How do you see me
How do you want to perceive me
Do we make too much of nothing
Or are nothings really something
Pay attention to our hearts
Intuition bends our minds

Rugs on puddles
Coats over oceans
Chivalry and ecstasy
Honesty and fantasy
Helplessness and shoulders
Grains of sand to wear down boulders
The light that shines into our eyes
Can also cruelly blind

Use me to cross that bridge of time
Use me to safely bring you home
Dress me
Clothe me
Keep me warm
I will safely bring you home
As love is redefined
As love is redefined.

5-21-92/2009/2011

AUTUMN'S FALL

When summer descends
Into autumn
And the leaves all fall into red
When the end is so beautifully clad
When he dresses his sibling trees
In harlotian flashes
Jesters' brilliance
A foolish optimist's epiphany
Coquettish, proud and sweetly round
How nice, how sweet the dance shoes sound
For all languages echo in unison
When its speakers in sleep and comas lie
The innocent in obedient anticipation
The weary to their relief

Awaiting, expecting
With little need for affected patience
Waiting 'til kingdoms come
Winter
Death
However called
With its preserving, blanketing, numbing mass
Stills and cools and kills
Camouflage painted in shades of refracted white
That poses for all purposes
A harbinger of purest light
No linen shroud hath dealt with same finesse
The utterness of this finality
Draped with such fanfare and festivity
For,
From the beginning,
We've feared too much the darkness.

Go, Solstice, go!

9-29-92/2009/2011/2012

WHY DO I HOLD ON?

And why do I hold on?
Because the empty skies
Are full of air
Because my lungs expand and seek
Though I can't look upon the sun
I let the warmth see me
And find the seas beyond me
Bend gently with a curve
Recollecting and imitating
The endless circle of the sun

And why do I hold on?
Because, oh,
Just because
Because two sets of marbled, crystal gazes
Look to me for all the answers
And because I still believe so much more in afters
Than I ever did in befores

And why do I hold on?
Because, oh,
The seeking
Is always ever so much sweeter
When the need is cause enough, atoned
Because I do not want to die alone
Nomadic
Self-contained

I have so much to write and say
I want to write
And need to speak
I want someone to not just hear me
I want someone to listen

And why do I hold on?
Because of air and skies and sun
Because of circles, eyes and sons

Because of afters and befores
Because I also need to be alone
Because I want to, on some day,
Understand and comprehend
Why happiness is a dialect
Abused by beggars, wisemen, foolish men
Who also strive to understand

5-16-92/2009/2011

TURN TURN

When shepherds become heroes
And shy becomes the rose
When a pagan's equinox could matter less
Then I'll be loving you

When the jester is the sage
And the wizened innocent come of age
When the dark horse rides unbridled fire
I'll still be loving you

When a mother first knows everything
And a father feels no fear
When the child needs no one to care
I'll still be needing you

When the earth's plates lose all tension
And every hurricane is hushed
When each snowflake's borne of random frost
I hope I'm holding you

When the galaxies come home
To where they all began
When the one explosion like a candle's flame
Draws from itself one final breath
Will you be loving me?

Turn turn turn turn
Will you be loving me?
Turn turn turn turn
Will you be needing me?
Turn turn turn turn
Will you be reaching out for me?
Reach out, reach out
Reach me, keep me
Will you be there with me?

1-6-93/2009/2011

COARSE VESPERS

If I were the only man
If a new-made god had had a hand
And named me like his son, Adam
How would I tell him no?
For,
Here I am
Fed perfect breath
Alive, alive to the last small cell
I watch the seas recede
And space is oh, so very deep
I cannot die
Cannot help but fly
My silver suit of armor
Weighs down the finest wings
So does my heart of gold
A bold man
New, noble, faith en-crutched
I'm floating
Or is this falling?
A spacewalk should last less than an hour
I've been on mine for days…

If only I were home again
If I just had a bed on which to land
If I could awake to see a familiar roof over my head
How could I want to go?
But
Here I bask
In perfect warmth
Insulated to the nth degree, preternaturally
Cocooned from total, infernal cold
Oh, god, it must be cold
A vacuum holds
Each last scrap of life
I am a captive saint of science
I am a good man, practiced and patient
But

Here I float
Dutiful and committed
Or am I falling
And should this question matter?
A spacewalk should have been a simple task
What questions can the dying ask?

If heaven is a science
Hell is then man-made
However well-intended
Paradise is child's play
History's voice grows hoarse
The lady sings her vespers coarse
Their meaning has grown old and frail
Distorted like a comet's tail
Heaven Science Belief and Knowledge
A long and winded trail

2-2-93/2009/2011/2012

BLACK BOX

Crash and burn
It feels too good
My secret sigh goes to the sun
And, damn it, it's gone way beyond
So listen to me
Listen
The broadcast prophet made his mark
And choice just grabbed hold of our throats
Pandora wears a vampire coat
And offers spoiled fruit
She was merely watching out for you
Her talons hanging to your back
A little pleasure, first, but then…

You strain to see beyond the edge
A tar pit of desire
The scream is lustful
Listen to it
Listen!
It's calling to the virgins' light
As black keeps oozing over night
Don't fear the sleep, then,
Shut your eyes
Your will see
Nothing, nothing, nothing
You will see nothing at all

Hello, hello
Oh, where is it am I going?
Choirboys pin their ribbons to their frocks
And the shepherds scream at frightened flocks:
Come crawling to me,
Sinners!
I took no poison but your wine
The bread, the manna, isn't mine
Good boys and girls, you're out of time
The silent can but cry

And sleep in lace and formal tails
And with ashes burn and cinders signed
Crosses, circles, trails benign
Seeking immortality in the ritual

Ten thousand cranes are looking back
Let's shoot them down, indeed
They're calling to us, warning us
Their cries sound too much like laughter
Why should I want to hold the skies
The curtain's weighted
Pull it
If fear is stoked to lose them then
And I am left with mere ragged edge
It would mean seeing
Nothing, nothing
It would mean seeing nothing at all.

Then petrified
Like some Darwinian outcast
Some plebian bug in amber cast
I will look in on you with future's disdain
And deign to appreciate the specimen
What a fine example we have here!
Why, you can look right through it, kids,
And you're knocking
And you're tapping
Will they be able to break your code?

Look inside
Looking back
See what in there flies
You will be given your own black box
Though others are sent to test the locks
Dark destiny shall make your bed
If all passengers should fall ill
Not a sound belies the panic
Too much enlightenment could prove too boring
As that would mean knowing, knowing, knowing

That would mean knowing
Too much about it all

1-22/30-93/2009/2011/2012

MONARCHS

Crucify the monarch
(Who's chasing butterflies?)
Crucify the monarch
(Who gets to set them free?)

Who's chasing butterflies
Who raises one small fist and cries
Crucify the monarch!
Who's capturing each fragile dream
Who's taking what can't seem to be
And making sure it doesn't stay that way
Nothing ever really changes
I do I have I want…
(Crucify the monarch…)
Who's chasing butterflies
Who's strapped convention to gentle wings
And set free the fragile monarchs
When jaded conviction
Is turned to upside down
Who'll step back inside the chrysalis
Immortality's cocoon
(Crucify the monarch…)
I will…
I have…
I have to do…
I want I want I want…

3-93/2011

THE BANNER OF HER LOVE

What does she speak to me
What legends are in her simple yes
So quietly she waits at night
She's learned to share me
As she's loved me
I am lost in her emerald skies
I breathe in the taste of a soul
So much like mine
She's so much mine
If only they all could know…

I want to fly the banner of her love
I want to tell the world
On the altar, lay her down
The sound of her sighs
The joy in her cries
She is the song I want to hear
Again, again
And again

How does she draw me in
What masterpiece takes fire in her hands
How can she know, how much I love
I touch the warm earth
And the cool heavens above
Each time in my arms I take her
I am the artist
I molded the clay
Sweet Aphrodite gave her life
The chance to step down to me
Into my waiting arms
I know now what love is for…

She whispers
Her breath plays across my eyes
Of a love and of a life
In awe of the sunrise deep inside

An angel in a peasant's guise

Simplicity deceives
And soft deception's mask we wear
The illusion of the storm we bear
Is reality
I'm so awake
In the wake of her giving and her taking
Our time apart is meaningless
I close my eyes
She's there
Some day for all
For all the crazy world to see…

3-11/18-92/ 2010/2011

I WANT TO DIE A KING (THE MONEY PIT)

I'll excavate my way
To the end of all my dreams
I'll slide its length
To rainbow's end
To bathe beneath the weight
Of the gold that waits for me
Of the silver, or so it seems
Of pearls that flow like fatty cream
Into my sacred cup

I'll thrash against the graves
That crash on shores as oceans' waves
Borne of wanton lust and glory
Of pirate's darkest dreams
I'll gladly drown, satiated
By the hand of cruelest, coldest seas
And kisses wet made just to please
A mermaid greeting, open armed
I'll have her next for dinner
Who needs a woman, so I'll say
When one can swim in boundless riches
The faithful want their answers
I want to die a king

Help me foist this sarcophagus
Lay it hastily aside
If it is for me to rape this Nova Scotian land
I'll do it tenderly
And I'll work in absolute silence
Without a single light
In this cavern of endless, ink-washed night
No man can serve as witness
If I am to die a king

Until I breach that tomb
Where ten oaks lie like sleeping giants
Before once more the surf comes rushing in

And swallows deep of me
The army ant I'll be retired
The last breath sucked whole from me
Explorer, thief, expired
I'll use *your* back to span my bridge
For no matter what, I want to die a king

Into the deep I go
One hundred and seventy swirling feet
A bit too close
To the likes of hell
Reminiscent of a Fury's spell
Where the gold of fools
Becomes the fuel
As wicked, wicked tales are told
Which, in my greed, I vow forever to believe
For I want to die a king!
How in my greed
I have decreed
I want to die a king!

5-27-92/2011/2012/12-19-2024

On Oak Island off Nova Scotia is a genuine historical mystery known as the Money Pit. It is said to hold the treasure of Captain William Kidd, the 17th century pirate, buried in a shaft sunk one hundred and seventy feet deep. Large flagstones cap its top. Every ten feet, a barrier of oak logs blocks the way. Digging beyond 90 feet opens a hidden channel to the sea, which floods the shaft. No one has ever reached the bottom of the Money Pit.

COINS TO CLOSE HIS EYES

I watched him walking down the street
I watched him nod his head to greet
Perfection of a studied sort
He counted out his courtesies
But left most in his pockets

I watched him open up the door
And take the stairs that led below
A stealthy breeze killed the one warm light
The shadows as yet did illuminate
In welcome, their dark arms opened wide

Something as sinister
As this man's smile
Holds me back
As all the while I watch, I wait
I quietly watch and wait

I watched him sign his name in ink
I watched him pause for once to think
He seemed to know just what to do
His plans as tailored as his suit

The faintest sound of coolest chain
Began to link him to the gold
That I once saw him kneeling to
Though none had fallen to the floor
H spoke the word, "Amen."

I was left with nagging, little questions:
What kind of sleep would solace him
What kind of peace could envelope him?
What should I take from this?

My quickened thoughts and fears took hold
As I was lead, entranced
Right through his open window

And left to float above his bed
To face direct his countenance
And in his face to read
The answer I to this day dread
For, there he sleeps
And there he lies
With a coin of gold atop each eye.

4-92/2009/2011/2012

JANE

I once knew all the words
And the melody was clear
But our time together
Faces bitter weather
Storms of circumstance
Tear asunder

Oh, God, how I want you, my sullen, brilliant Master
But her shadows whisper, sifting, maddened
Up there, up there, in her high tower
Locked up within my heart
Clasped as such, to her hollow breast
Are we all your hapless prisoners?

Sands of time fall silent
My senses long to hear
The howling trees, the angry seas
My longing brings me to my knees
Please, teach me how to sing

You came here innocent
Your gaze remains unchanged
You ask was she the one, my love,
Was she the stars, the moon, the sun
Lord, if I only knew

Forget my troubled past
Hold me to your looking glass
Let me see myself through you
Let me see myself in you

Oh, Jane,
A shadow bathed in light
A slip of heather from the moors
I hold a quiet passion, love
Smooth as a river stone
Deep as a sailor's dream

Oh, Jane,
Your smile is all I need
Your kisses make me now complete
The quiet passion, my dear one
Will free us as we roam
And let us call this world our home

I let myself fall short
When I promised her my life
What I have signed away
Has scarred me and it haunts me now
I have become the prey

Someday the walls will rush around us
And crash onto the ground
Then cleansed by grace of wind and fire
And bled until we've drowned
I will promise to find you then

Oh, Jane,
A woman and a child
A leaf to catch the rain
I hold a quiet passion, love
That calls to you in vain
Can you hear my cry, my love?
Oh, Jane,
Don't turn your mind away
Don't trade your love for misplaced pride
I want you at my side
No other soul will do
I want you at my side
Our tears will bring the rain in time
And you will hear me sing
Oh, Jane…

1992/2009/2011/2012

HELL-BENT TO HEAVEN

Who makes the time of day
When emotion overkills
Passion's perfect waves
My hold is true
Hang on
Hang on
I'll take you to a higher place
And watch the pleasure in your face
Ave, ave…

Believe in me, I pray
It's in everything you say
Accept my dare
Try on these wings
If we're hell-bent to heaven
We're halfway there
Promise me
Show me where
Show me
Show me
Show me

Slow motion overtakes
Dreary nights and endless days
The speed of light
Will have its day
And every moment that has ever been
Will be mere distance
Between our kisses
Kisses
Kisses
Kisses

I'm hell-bent to heaven
I've left my seraph in the dust
The cherubs sucked upon the froth

Eden has nothing
On this circumstance
Where every question we dare ask
Will find in time its answer
In all befores
Before the after
After all
The aftermath
Is sweeter for the bitter

Look where it's taken us
Look where we're going
Keep your eyes open
Wide, my love
Wide, look out
Wide, look in
Wide, the door we rend asunder

9-8-92/2009/2011/2012

SHE WANTS

She wants to be a princess
She dies a death for every wish
Hoping, hoping
Please, please come true
Please save me from divided blue
Call me your girl divine
She wants to be a princess

She wants to live forever
She chases down the wind
Flying, always crying
Please slow down, she sobs
Please fold me in your tempest tide
Don't let me drown, just let me ride
I want to live forever

Who needs another angel
When she comes into the room
Why pray another word
When heaven's in a prince's arms
Descend into my heart, she sighs
Descend into my heart

She wants to be an actress
The one they pay to see
Every, every, everything's
In every note she tries to sing
To pull inside and draw way out
Every woman who has ever lived
She wants to play them all

But sister's baking bread
Another's cradled two soft, sleepy heads
She wonders, should she be doing this,
In lieu of dishes
Casting wishes
Should goals fit inside their picket fences

Do doors closed to tidy rooms
Hide a make believe stripped on all defenses?

12-92/2009/2011

A SCORCHING KIND OF COOL

You've built a room
Without a single window
You put me in a corner
Up against the wall
There are too many questions
There's a shortage of good answers
What can I say
What can I do?
Your pretty, practiced attitude
Is a scorching kind of cool

Hey, I don't need
Your infantile wisdom
I gave you everything
And now you just want more
How can there be enough
When what we have has cost too much
The texture's rough
The surface's raw
It is a sugar-coated kind of cruel

Lend me for once
Your cutting words
I need to cut these bars
Untie the binds
That hold me still
That still hold me to you
Please, let me go
You go, too.

Your pretty, practiced attitude
Is a scorching kind of cool
Your imagery of gratitude
Is a sugar-coated cruel
Your great pretense at aptitude
Of empathy, of respect
Is something crafted, tailor-made for willing, mindless fools

And I, my dear, am no fool.

6-27-92/2009/2011

THE MONSTER

Child-spider, weaving webs of wishes
In her sleep
Scope-minded, sees so far beyond
The olde worlde
Mirrored, smooth horizons
Hung in aging, ancient halls
Not to look into, but look past
There's a message lost within itself
Found on the other side of darkest seas
What monsters lie within?

Child-bride of warfare's inane circumstance
A crooked cross wasn't meant for you
You understood there had been a someone else
Long before the apparition
Broke the fickle, daylight ties that bound
You to your basal obligation
Dead flags fly like streamers now
And webs keep spinning 'round and 'round.

Man-child defined by a worn-out humankind
When dreamers, heroes and innocents
Yet dared in all believe
With faith kept by faith afire
With all the unknowns borne of such desire
Believers left, all of you, to your best unkempt demise
The boatman said there'd be a price
When across the darkest seas you were tossed
The monster was left behind

Or so you thought
Once the next one's face was slapped

2-10-93/2009/2011/2-20-2013

HAND OVER FIST

Listen to him...
What a diff'rence does it make
It pulls a strong man in
Brittle shackles on his wrist
Hand over fist
He fights it off
Hand over fist
He wants to make it end
Arm wrestling with an angel
Mercy-twisted vengeance
The signs were in the murky skies
The questions in the wind-swept sighs
The gypsy had no answer

Hand over fist
There's an infant in the ring
A Tarzan wannabe
The type the loneliest ones long to love
Hand over breast
What reason is left
But a foolish sort of wisdom
Something angry teachers hide behind
Each time innocence lifts the lid
Oh, but the demons had such sweet, sweet smiles
What promises they whispered
What type of truths betrayed

Hand over fist
Evolution's own confusion
Oh, man, procreate
It's the process that inebriates
Hand over fist
Over in a heated flash
Hand over clenched and fickle fist
A Madonna for your finish
You who think you have to win
To come in second is to be damned

Society requires it
Oh, man, what a man he's now become
The loneliest of creatures toss their greying manes
Beautiful to behold, in memory at least
Shallow waters, iced in minutes
Hand over fist
To hell with all the rest.

2-19-93/2009/2011

THE HANCOCK RED

She wore a pearl of crimson
Like anger crystallized
A token of the time
That Fate herself was born
Borne unlike the beauty won
Borne of passionate,
Blood-red seething
Wreathed in vines entwining
Blood-red roses
Losing petals to a blood-red dawn
Carved and cut
To satisfy the need
For human-hued geometry
And its penchant for opulence
Then hidden through the epochs
(so long and oh, so dreary)
Until a slave reached down and pulled
From its hubris upholstered berth
And It cried out against the light

Like an odalisque
Too perfect for her cage
He'll bed you in a velvet gown
The oil and sweat of eight hundred thousand
Made you as a technicality better than all the rest
So let him build you a better nest
Though keep your song to yourself

You are a Helen
Who watches from her virgin tower
Would someone kill to have you?
Would someone die to keep you?
Are you in love with your own desire
A token to others so unlike you
Or would you rather lose yourself
Amongst your simpler brothers
In an anonymous river bed?

4-9/10-92/2009/2011

The Hancock Red, a diamond weighing .95ct, sold for $880,000 to a Sultan in April of 1987, a record price per carat to date.

CITIZENS & FOOLS

Citizens and fools
Go ahead and write your rules
A homing pigeon comes back home
We're honing skills we barely own
Too little wisdom for our science
Citizens and fools

Citizens and fools
You say your head hurts, mine does too
From listening and wagering
Wages, welfare and futile wars
Citizens and fools

Put your small hands to your hearts
Promise life before it starts
Let us end it as we choose
Blend the colors in graying schools
It's only minds
And minds are yours
Blissful, empty, angry hungry
Citizens and fools

Citizens and fools
Caste is the system, dressed and cool
As breezy promised streets of gold
Have long since, long since, long been sold
The buyers have no face or name
Just citizens like you

Citizens and fools
Line your loved ones down to rest
In gardens filled with monuments
Plastic flowers, paper flags
Faded, jaded reds and blues

Citizens and fools
Designer labels, foreign cars

Billions seeking life on Mars
While babies linger on the streets
And matter less than nothing
What does their substance matter
When only hunters gather
And the lowly are consumed
Citizens and fools
Citizens and fools

6-23-92/2011

A BLUER SHADE OF BLUE

I know New England's nice
Each hill is in its place
The sky is touched by upright steeples
Looks down upon its well-bred people
I know New England's nice

I've seen the ocean too
Its angry shade of blue
I saw a rain-soaked, hungry cloud
Reach down and with an angry shout
Take in the last of trembling sky
And from up high
I heard it, too
A flash of laughter light its fuse
I've seen the ocean too

And now I'm on my way
I should get there today
My mind is wound 'round silver heartstrings
My mem'ries tug like worn out shoestrings
They pull me on my way

I've seen the mountains too
Bathed in majestic hues
I've heard an echo, mountain-framed
I think it tried to call my name
A part of me is still out there
For all I know it's like a stage
Carved from the finest rocks of Age
I've seen the mountains too

The further west I go
The more the sky takes on
The earth-bound shine of old turquoise
The sky-bound hawk he watches, poised
And nods his head my way

A bluer shade of blue
And ever-reaching view
It moves beyond my breathless self
The pebble skipped off of the edge
The world that serves, a heavy shelf
From which I need to choose
A bluer shade of blue

1991/2011

IRON CLAD

Let's rock tonight
And storm the walls
Let's move this out
Shake down the halls
I've got an energy
To spend
Oaken barrels full of gold
Grab some of it with me
And try my sweet surprise
We're movin' through the dark of night
Until we hit the next sunrise

I'm a 21st century knight
It is my will that's iron clad
I wear my dark desire
Like a suit of virgin steel
Horsepower's at my will
And it's taking me straight down to hell
So lady fair
Entwine your fingers in my hair
And tempt me
Tell me
Are you my Magdelene
Or my Jezebel?

I want you here
To play to me
I need you now
Your luxury
Pull down this guard
And make me purr
With lethal stroke, the dragon slayed
We're wingin' it through the dark of night
Until we hit the next sunrise

Let's dance tonight
The music's fine

Let's take a dip
The water's wine
We're too physical to rest
Acrobats or jesters
Climb up with me
Know ecstasy
Fly through the night
Until we hit the next sunrise

1991/92/2011

ISLE OF UNKNOWN

Who are you
What have you seen and done
Whose arms have held you in the night
Who cradled you at birth

Am I just one small piece of lyric prose
Some poetry for you to spin
Am I the fool for thinking that
You might have been the one

Cross the river of forgetfulness
To the Isle of Unknown

Do you think I'll love you better
If you're kept a mystery
Illusion stays unbroken
Disappointment lays unspoken

Should I paint a brave face on
Pull my bridges in, go on
Should I deify or realize
Our end has now begun

Where you'll have gone
No one will ever know
Lochs are unnecessary
The path is deep
Sea creatures are mere folklorists' dreams

How we watched on glassy plains
Longed for a break in all that stillness
Sonic echoes or merely whistles
Crimson moons are merely apples

Upon your Isle of Unknown
Only you know who you are
You recede

You're fading faster
Into the mindlessness of fog
A warlock, no, you are a traveler now
Joined to an endless, human train

Upon your Isle of Unknown
Is this how you'll be remembered
You're just one person
So like so many others
You are so much like me
In the end, we're merely human

7-28-92/2011

ODE TO COOPERIAN IDEAL

A shadow lies
In eyes that otherwise
Shine so lucid and so bright
A nocturnal soul drives you
Yet you falter
Desire distracted momentarily
But your spirit cannot help
But wander
You ask why I should stay
I ask you
Why should you not leave me now?
Do you not know that I will wait?
Never to bask in you again
Is not possible in this realm
You who reach for the sun
Are yourself my sun

Your are a free, partaking man
In a god-forsaken, wild land
The ancient mountains your divan
The tangled, untamed woods your bed
The primitive palace offers rest
You lay yourself beneath its trees
I will in spirit place myself
Right there, my love, beside you
What gives you strength will guide me too
As I wait, as I seek you
You who are the sanctuary,
You who seek the arrow's North
Are you, yourself, my True North

So be on your way now, my scout
I will, my love, soon follow
To stay behind would be a death
A half-life, dark and hollow

The scholars harvest history

Its branches scored in wet, red lines
Across the shoulders, backs and necks
Of all the victor's losers
I will read this fable to our children
Lest in time they might forget
The gift of our shared memories
Tall tales borne of this wild country
Called by shadowed men Ken-tah-ten
You who must now wander off
To roam far and deep and on and on
This crude, magnificent, earthly shelter
Is room enough for us
Enjoined in time, so it shall be
'tis room enough for longing
You who call this tundra home
Are yourself my home

1993/2011/2012

RAINDANCE

Come on
Let loose
Back off from the arid road
Others travel
Step out of line and out of your shoes
It's a different way for us to move
A distance drumbeat curls your senses
My heart throbs to your body's rhythms
Ever faster
Ever faster
Listen with me
Feel it

Feel it coursing through your veins
And join me in this primal groove
Shed the last of your emotions
They are mere dregs of rags
Leave them on the ground, my dear
Let inhibitions go!
I will lead you in a wicked waltz
The vixen teachers have well taught us
We turn
We spin
Sleek and black
New-borne, native
Jungle cats
Serpentine entwined

I'll teach you all the steps I know
Everything that's old is new
And if it's strange, it's wonderful
You'll get used to it, I know
This raging sound
These pulsing coils
Urge us
Urge us
Urge us on

Follow me
Now follow
Now come on,
Come on, come on to me
Come to me, now
Come on

1989/1992/2011

ODE TO MAGELLAN

What more do you want of me
Three minutes more so let me go
I've found a way out
Through heaven's door
I'd like to see
What's out there just for me
Haven't I done enough?
And now you ask
Of me one last mission
A kamikaze swan-song epilogue
To fill your journals
Complete your logs
Can't you just see
I want to be
Out there
There, in the cold waters
You call night
Some call dark matter

No, it won't do
Silly, wishful, sentient me

I'll go and read your clouds
Your planet's pretty, poisoned shroud
Will need to be enough for me
So it shall pass
Three minutes more….

11-94/10-2011

XMAS

As the innocent and ignorant
Speak in voices caught up yet
An octave lifted into the air
Prepared along in celebration
Of religious, dutiful permutations
Bent on all the glittered and besparkled
Things that shine and preen
When Constantine decreed
And pulled his peasants to their knees
Laid claim to a little peace and harmony
A moment in which all guns would cease
A bowl of broth for the old, old man
It is, I guess, okay with me
I can accept the context
Though the acting out is poorly spent
When night outweighs the day
And hours are stretched and tied
Papers, pens and images bound together
As crass as they are benign

There's holiness, indeed
In every baby's fragile breath
Whether borne of lust
Or duty-bound love of promises
Little answers to little prayers
End the silence that follows close
On the heels of moans and laughter spent
The miracle, the divine creativity
The animalistic biology
Are one within each other
For we are artists
We are lovers.

12-16-95/2011/2012

DONKEY-HOHTEY

Your lips crack
And your nose bleeds
What noble notion, martyr's dream
Flat-line songs, fools' rhetoric
Are less
No more
Than bitter words flung out by junior wisemen

Say it quiet
Whisper to the mountains
Let the softest words slide
Where they fall might yet fill the void
And flow to the beaches of the soul
But if she doesn't want to listen
Let her go
Let stillness fill that hole
Then go, then go, then go, then go
There's bound to be some table round
With a place still set for you.

9-29-92/2012

THE LOFT

It is windy out tonight
Webs loosened from the rafters
Play across my face and eyes
Seeing less and less
Hearing yet the lonely cry
Who lies protected from those winds
Those restless, listless winter winds
There is snow outside
But the cold is far away
Its strands cannot sift through

Summer sun and its standard green
Well-intended invitations
Swept-up sheaves of last year's wheat
The field mice and the birds
Though hungry, can still look
They are thin and they remember
Endless, temporary warmth
They know the earth alive and kind
Primitively stoic
Strong yet unprotected

In the loft
There is security
The illusion of permanence hangs on
The incense of young ones lost in love
The essence wafts beyond
Whisps that curl into a poet's words
Any heart would want to hear

Shingles break and fall
Hinges creak
As do the doors
Torn open wide in the search
For any reassurance from the sun
Cold, cold rain slides down
Weathered panes

Gathering stars
Whether pain
Or growth
Overlooking the simplicity of angled form
Proverbial guard against the ever-expanding
It's a nothingness that lurks
Over each last loft
Folly, those presumptive firmaments of men
Builders
Ants

When night clouds gather
And brush the webs from my seeking eyes

...oh, but deceit comes gently

1-12-94/10-2011/2012

VII. Studio E – the Lyrics

SPIRIT OF CHRISTMAS – the poem

Christmas Spirit
Open up our hearts and
Caring, sharing
Like the light of all the stars
Which show us all the way
Where the Baby Jesus lay
A herald angel sings
The message quickly takes to wing
One holy Baby's birth
Brings peace, good will to all on Earth

Christmas Spirit
Candles in the window
Glowing, showing
To the people here below
That love can conquer all
God's Son was sent there for
A simple manger bed
To cradle precious Baby's head
We sing His lullabye
And though He sleeps we see He smiles

Christmas Spirit
Our eyes must open wider
Singing, laughing
Joyous notes swell with the tide
Of songs to Christ's new glory
One simple, perfect story
The shepherd boy does tell
The light that dances on the bells
Reflects a hope so new
That shines beneath the heaven's blue

Christmas Spirit
Be with us every day
And ever giving
Guide us in thy way

Let Jesus' birth keep in us
The light of God's good promise
The greatest gift we've ever known
The love of God as He has shown
Will warm our souls forever
Rejoice, all ye, in boundless measure.

1991

SPIRIT OF CHRISTMAS – the carol
Performed by the St. Luke United Methodist Church choir, Indianapolis, Indiana, Jan. 2005

Spirit of Christmas
Open up our hearts
Caring and sharing
Like the lights of all the stars
That show us all the way
Where baby Jesus lay
A herald angel sings
The message quickly takes to wing

Spirit of Christmas
Candles in the window
Glowing and showing
To all the children here below
That love can conquer all
God's Son was sent there for
A simple manger bed
To cradle precious Baby's head

Spirit of Christmas
Our voices lifter higher
Singing and laughing
The joyous notes swell with the tide
Of songs to Christ's new glory
One simple, perfect story
The shepherd boy does tell
The light that dances on the bells

Spirit of Christmas
Be with us every day
Ever giving
Guide us in thy way
Let Jesus' birth keep in us
The hope of God's good promise
The greatest gift we've known
The love of God as He has shown

1991-92/7-15-2004

SPIRIT OF CHRISTMAS revisited

Spirit of Christmas
Open up our hearts
Caring and sharing
By the light of heaven's stars
That show us all the way
Where innocence still lay
A herald angel sings
The message quickly takes to wing

Spirit of Christmas
Candles in the window
Glowing and showing
To all the children here below
That love can conquer all
A son was sent there for
When simple manger beds
Were all that cradled baby's head

Spirit of Christmas
Our voices lifted higher
Singing and searching
For harmony to hold in time
A song of new-found glory
And solace in the story
That shepherd boys still tell
Of peace that rings with every bell

Spirit of Christmas
Be with us every day
Ever giving
Guide us in thy why
Let every birth keep in us
The gift of mankind's promise
When souls like seeds are sown
For hope to blossom, breathe and grow

December 17, 2012
Version for peace and hope, post Newtown shooting
Available on YouTube

LIFE STEPS IN

Are there miles in our weary steps
I do believe there are
Is there music in our tired words
I do believe there is
Oh, memory
What a sweet and soulful thing
That keeps my heart a'beating
That keeps me remembering.

It's not with just
A little fear
That I see the magic fly
Our hearts begin to touch the ground
And your voice becomes another sound
Of just another man around
Fireworks fade
Ok, so they go
The lights in our eyes soon grow dim
Life steps in
I guess it's alright
And remember to kiss you goodnight.

And has it been too many years
I do believe it has
And have I cried too many tears
I do believe I have
Oh, promise me
To be somehow the one I knew
When I first fell in love
When my heart first found you.

Is this what life owes folks like us
Oh, God, what if it does
Is this love what's due me then
I guess I'm paid in full
Oh, come with me
Take my hand as I move on

And take a slow and steady walk
Please take my love for what it's worth
I hope
It was worth enough

1991-92

LULLABYE – SHIP OF DREAMS

Ship of dreams
A cloud of memories
Cradle swaying
Lullabye

Feathered tiptoe
Blanket 'round you
Mama kisses
Day good-bye

Fairy tales
And Never-never land
Take you oh, so far away

Teddy bears
And White Horse Indian
Bid you welcome
Can you play?

Baby sweet
My little everything
Little sweet song
That I sing

In your bed now
Know security
Is the prayer
That I bring

Lullabye now
Baby lullabye
Even angels kiss goodnight

On your sweet brow
Baby sleep now
'til the break
Of morning light

1989

IMAGINE

Imagine me
With you
No more cares or worries too
Just me
And you
The minstrel marks with his sweet tune
The rhythm of
Our kisses
And our glances mirrored there
The motion in
Our dances
Taking chances filled with dare

Hands that open
Hands that care
Hands that hold each other's hearts
Until our souls
Will fly beyond
This room and touch the skies above

Imagine me
With you
Because that's how I want you to
Just me
And you
In you alone my world is full
The times to come
The tears
The conquering of our fears
And though love's cost
Is high
You've got to pay to reach the sky

Eyes that open
Wide to see
The silver edge to all our dreams
And how the night

Bends to the day
To guide these lovers on their way

Imagine me
With you
No longer scared of what is true
When truth defines the dream
And your realness is all I see
And your realness is all I see
For what is love is all it seems
I love the love you bring to me
Thank God for bringing you to me
And let me always have in you
What I could ever be to you
What I could ever be to you
What I could ever be to you
Imagine me with you…

1991

PIROUETTE

No
Don't go
Let's call this night our own
Come stay
Let's make
This hour just the first
Come move
With me
No, let's not just rehearse
Let's make love
Let's move as one
Let's greet the sun together

Let me lead you in a pirouette
In a lover's downward spiral
For is not the best love
A dance we dream to dance?
Is not the best love
Like a dance,
Like a dance?

Here
By me
This room is now our world
Touch me
Softly
Like a lover would
Come close
More still
No, I really think we should
Make this night
Of love tonight
Let's cheat the Fates together

Let me lead you in a pirouette
In a lover's downward spiral
For is not the best love

A dance we dream to dance?
Is not the best love
Like a dance,
Like a dance?

See
In me
All that you'd ever need
This dance
Of chance
The ace is in our hands
Kiss me
Love me
No, this is not an act
It's our moves
And our rules
Let's warm our world together

Why,
We ask
Should we want to know
How long
How far
What does our future hold?

Touch my hands
To your lips
The choreography becomes perfection

Not a word
This is eternity
We're already there
Let me take you farther

Anywhere....

1991-92

EVERYONE

Everyone
Who should ever be
With me
Is here
Right now
This moment
Shall hold in time
Perfection
On my mind

Every hour
That did ever pass
In time
Has come
Right now
This midnight
Shall always toll
Its sweet
And timeless tune

Every where
That I've ever wanted to be
Is here
'round me
Tonight
Galaxies are melted skies
Reflected
In your shining eyes

Every love
I could ever love
Could break
Could heal
In you
My passion has captured me
With you I am finally free

To each
His own
To everyone, another
To me
To you
For me
For you

1991/2009

GUN METAL GHOST

Gun metal ghost
Skirting fragments from the past
Gravity wants to pull you close
You use it just to throw yourself
Onto another path
We're listening, we're listening
We're leaning to the edge
Where darkness is complete
Infinity the norm
The sun is now a cool pin prick
A light without a warmth

Gun metal ghost
Cutting off the frequency
You tease us with your language games
You please us with the visions gained
Beyond what children see
It's what we want, secretly
It's what we'll need, eventually
When night becomes the day
And time rewinds its hands
The earth is now irrelevant
A pleasant memory

Take mental note
Of where you've been in this young flight
Your wings of wax, no science molds
Don't melt with good intention
Or brittle, break them off
Your robot arms are not enough
Your vision quest requires
As you're wading through the mire
Prehistoric soup
The older children turn away
Say good-bye, now go your way

Gun metal ghost

Chasing silver fish and flies
Caught in your nets like Spanish coins
Dim rainbows lit by thirteen watts
Then a batt'ry of a watch
Until it's just the energy
As reaching out, two fingers touch
The Father and His work
Infinity the norm
Your sun has long since disappeared
And so you seek one more

What kind of love will you want to make
Whose empty house will you haunt tonight
The tattered webs of angels' gowns
Frame the windows
And the doors
Looking for a home,
Oh, no
You're happy where you are

Where are you?

2-22/23-92

To the Voyager II. Don't we wish we could follow and see too....

JUST ANOTHER WAY OF DYING

See the dancer like a swan
The dance was not enough
(Or was it far too much?)
Write for her a requiem
It's just another way of dying

See the flower in the rain
Her tears come from above
(Why does she die of thirst?)
Tuck away a memory
Sense the lavender in her sighing

Why is this pain intensifying?
Missing you is just another way of dying

Feel the heartstrings cut in two
The harmony was lost
(The sound is long since gone)
Hear the scratches in the wall
It's a fright'ning way of listening

Feel the fragments cut like glass
What diamonds are as bright
(What stars yet pierce the night)
If these hours never end
Then forever I'll be crying

Missing you so much, the pain
Is just another way of dying
Are you the saint
They sent to save
Are you the resurrection
Or am I falling
While I'm flying
Missing you
Is just another way of dying

Know the secrets, read the signs
Small words are not enough
(My poetry is rough)
My body is a paperback
Read 'til my pages fall apart

Know I need you, I can't help
The way I feel tonight
(The taste I had remains)
Leaves me starving evermore
It's just another way of dying

Near midnight tolls a soulful sound
The haunting of my sleep
Though it's no dog-eared photograph
It's the image that I keep
I just can't see you soon enough
I just can't see you soon enough
I just cant see you
Soon
Enough

2-28-92

ELLE 'DORA

Elle 'Dora
Desperado, lady fine
Twist and like a rose, entwined
Silken streamers breathe and climb
Over dancing arms and legs
In language all the ancients understood

In language
All the ancients
Understood

Elle 'Dora
Sensuality reprised
Victorians always closed their eyes
For you're not of their kind
Oh, 'Dora, I think not
Although I'm sure the ancients understood

Although
I'm sure
The ancients
Understood

Elle 'Dora
Take me to your show tonight
Dance against the fire light
A wand'ring butterfly
And let me lift you high
To steps the ancient lovers understood

To steps
The ancient lovers
Understood

Elle 'Dora
Your silhouette defines
In golden shades of white

Uncertain was your gift
When a flying scarf was death
The lady left her silent stage too soon

The lady
Left her silent stage
Too
Soon

4-21-92

HIYALAYA

I'm looking for a bit of twine
Some poles, some wooden planks
I'm looking for a soul like yours
Cut from a cloth like mine

I want to build a boat for you
An ark of triumph to this dream
The ocean's full of tears and brine
Reflections fathomless

I see our love a journey bend
I see it as you'd want me to
The sunset sky is ours to hold
To fold into the water's blue

Let's travel every current's path
Let's see the world as ours
This globe I hold in my small hands
A marble in your sands

Why should we feel a sadness
For what we cannot share
Not everyone will have this chance
Not everybody cares

I want to build a boat for you
Hiyalaya is its name
An ark of triumph to our dreams
The trade winds call our names

May the sirens sing to you
As they comb their golden hair
Let the sun kiss soft your eyes and face
For evermore, evermore

Hiyalaya, come with me
Hiyalaya, finally free

Our souls are sails that fill the air
The cloth is one, the same
Hiyalaya, find a sea
Hiyalaya, named for me
Our days are journeys marked by time
My harbour's in your eyes
Hiyalaya, blood-red skies
Hiyalaya, seagulls cry
At dawn she sails with morning light
A dream in brilliant white
        2-14-92
HYMN TO HER – the poem

Mona, mona mine
Lady, lady, soft and fine
Mia, mia, let me gather you in
Somewhere, somewhere far from here
There's an extra sensual infinity
I'm searching, searching
Finding, finding
Mona, mona mine

Oh, Gloria, Gloria
Let me kiss each fingertip
Say lady, lady, curvaceous reliquary
The incense in your smile
I want to burn in your sweet fire
I hope each tear you cry
Anoints and blesses
Poignant moments, memories
Oh, lady, lady mine

1-14-93/2009

HYMN TO HER – the song

Sensual infinity
I'm searching, searching
This is where you'll find me
Mona, Mona mine

Mona, Mona, Mona mine
Lady, lady, soft and fine
Mia, mia, gather me in
Somewhere far from here

Gloria, Gloria
Take my kisses one by one
Until we cross the edge of time
Mona, Mona mine

Mona, Mona, Mona mine
Lady, lady, soft and fine
Mia, mia, gather me in
Somewhere far from here

Sensual infinity
I'm searching, searching
This is where you'll find me
Oh, lady, lady fine

Mona, Mona, Mona mine
Lady, lady, soft and fine
Mia, mia, gather me in
Somewhere far from here

I want to burn in your sweet fire
And smell the incense in your smile
I want to taste each tear you cry
Oh lady, lady fine

Mona, Mona, Mona mine
Lady, lady, soft and fine

Babe I'm sure you'd like my moves
Say your name the way you do
Say it again when I call you
Say your name the way you do

Let me turn the lights way down
Let me turn your voice way up
Meet me in my room tonight
Mix our shadow in the light
Eight to midnight, baby
Eight to midnight

1992

THE CRAZY I COULD BE

Whisper softly in my ear
Words are the silken sounds I feel
Lay your breath against my cheek
Touch me in the light I see
Feed me the fire
Rise up in me
I love the crazy I could be
About you
About you

Keep me endless in this place
I hate the thought of time in space
Infinity, eternity
Are part of your embrace
Rise to the tides
Ride with the storm
I am the ashes and the warmth
Within you
Within you

You are the sky above me
A heaven with no ceiling
I am sinner on my knees
I am a swimmer in your seas
I'm lost in you
And so far gone
I am the harbor with my arms
Around you
Around you

Lose me in your gaze tonight
Seduction sparkles in your eyes
Make me your own, it is my will
Take everything I have instilled
Make me forget
Break ev'ry rule
I am the path into your soul

I found you
I found you

You found me

1992

I LIKE THESE KINDS OF BLUES

I like these kinds of blues
No ocean rolling 'way from me
They're no one's eyes
No need for endless seas

I like these kinds of blues
Wind-swept feelings, if they are
My heart is mine
No need to worry now

So, go,
Ocean go
And fly
You empty skies
Go, thoughts and fears
Leave my mind
You won't find
No more tears

Kaleidoscopic view of me, too few
I like these kinds of blues…
There's never enough of whatever to go around
I like these kinds of blues…
Kaleidoscopic view of me, of you
I like these kinds of blues
I like these kinds of blues…

7-28-92

SHE SAID, "PLAY CHICAGO"

In a flash, she was there
In a flash, she was gone again
In the brightness of the instant
She said,
"Play Chicago"
There and then
He fell
In love

And now
He dreams
And now
He plays
And how the silver points of sound his flute relays
Are like the daggers to his heart
Because her image burned too bright
Blonde hair, green eyes
She said,
"Play Chicago"
There and then
He fell
In love

Out there, on the corner
Out there, in the traffic
His craziness is just the logic of a lunacy
That dawns when the sun sits right above the moon
And the moment coincides with endless ages
When all such loves roll
Into one
And all what's lost falls like pennies from above
So he plays his flute to fill the skies again
She said, "Play Chicago"
There and then
He fell
In love

"Play Chicago"
There and then he fell in love.

Dedicated to the street-corner musician who played his flute to the Michigan Avenue shoppers, even though they were not the ones who were supposed to hear.

5-3-92

FORGET ABOUT ME

I'd like to forget, if just for a while
I'd like to fly away
A solitary satellite
My arms held open wide

I'd like to watch the world go by
And watch the days unwind
I'd play this little trick on time
Erase the sadness from my eyes

An epitaph for you to read
Engraved by all my fears
A shadow of the smiles I smiled
Deluded by my tears

Where was it that I'd gone to
Where is it that I'd been
What stray halo found its way to me
And softened up my sins
Nostalgia holds what's left of me
And mem'ry keeps in clear
A nutshell for the times at hand
Encapsuled by the years

I'd like to forget, if just for a while
I'd like to fly away
And find that secret, solemn place
Where night turns into day

Then, satisified, at least for now
I'd go back home, and carry on
Wondering how easily
The bittersweet has gone

An epitaph for you to read
Engraved by all my fears
A shadow of the smile I smiled

Diluted by my tears

Where was it where I'd gone to
Where it is that I'd been
What stray halo found its way to me
And softened up my sin
Nostalgia holds what's left of me
And mem'ry keeps it clear
A nutshell of the times at hand
Encapsuled by the years
  7-14/22-92

THE HAUNTING

I'm prey to quiet moments
When thoughts ring home like mourning bells
The sounds of sadness pull me in
Forgetfulness release me
Everything I see
I see in the context of retrospect
The story of my life plays backwards
White on black
Wicked words from within
Memory go
Please go away
And pull your shadows in
Let me swim across his river, then

I hear her calling to me
In words so soft they touch me there
The sheets become the shroud she wears
The eyes of night still want me
Everyone I know
Becomes less of what I wanted once ago
Reality warps perspective
Wearing thin
The name she calls, calls me from within
Make the night
Please, go away
For the light of day
Makes it easier to find my way

I know I should know better
That years of time will heal the pain
No taunting words of false resolve
I've got nothing left to gain
And now all I want
I want in the context of retrospect
It's become to hard to move beyond
In this dream
Deep sea strokes instead of steps

Caught in the dive
Down to the blue
Bass strings pluck my heart
Let me sing to this empty room

I'll play to quiet moments
With thoughts awash like ocean waves
And castles built on shifting sands
Emptiness inside me
It's possible she'll hear
It's possible my love's still near

I lay my hands upon the table round
And cry out
Open up the windows, lay aside
Reason tonight
Seasons tonight
Spring summer winter's fall
Open up my mind to hear her call

3-9-92

DON'T

Don't reach for me
I never think of you
When days are black
And nights are blue
I've never wanted you

Don't call to me
Don't make me remember
What's memory
A spell on me
Apprentice magic, yeah

Don't weave me to your coat
Don't line me in your silk

Don't say my name
It's like a song you wrote
What's music then
You played me when
The music went too far

Don't promise me
Words that cut like winter winds
What trick of time
That edge is mine
I'm falling of it, yeah

Is there any differrence
Are emotions instruments?

I never think of you
Only never is a lie
I never want to see you
But I want you to try
I never should've loved you
My soul stretched out above you
My sky was full of you

8-29-92

NAME THIS HURRICANE

I've crossed temptation's line
Heard thunder in her cries
Now, star-crossed,
Star-struck
I've fallen from the skies
You're mine tonight
Let's ride the night
There's a comet laughing with delight

Oh, what a storm is love
What a storm
Is love

I'm in the darkened woods
Canopied with leaves
Now, hunter,
Hunted
Don't run from me
In time, my sweet
It's all complete
There's an arrow looking for your heart

Oh, what a quest is love
In this storm
Of love

My eyes take in the world
And search the wild seas
Let me, please
Release you
You've got me on my knees
And this is where
I want to be
There's a calm light dancing in your eyes
Still water's running deep

Oh, what a storm is love

What a storm
Is love

It's like some crazy carousel
Going round and round and round and round and round
I'm reeling with emotion
Avoiding solid ground

I want to feel this hurricane
And name it after you
I want to feel this hurricane
And name it after you

6-92

ECLIPSE

Close your eyes
Against the time
In front of day
Pretend it's night
Silhouette
The brightness in
The sickle of
A moon worn thin
A minute then
A minute gone
Gone until 2017

The image burned the foolish eye
Don't peer at it too closely, boy
You just might see everything
And see how,
Somehow,
It's still nothing
And see somehow it's still nothing

Let ignorance pull you on
If it pulls you on
Let ignorance pull you on
If it pulls you on
Some people call it blind ambition
Some people call it faith
Some people call it blind ambition
Some people call it faith

A prisoner
Of jealous skies
The sun can't hold
Though it tries
In shadowed truths
Are held the lies
Of foolish thoughts
And shallow smiles

A minute then
A minute gone
Until it finds you once again
Again

1992

COME, CHILD, KATIE

Come, child, Katie
I knew her once some long ago
Come, child, through a chamber door
Cold, cold creatures scurry through dark long agos
Curry woven patterns in her hair

Oh, orphans
Katie say what lucky ones they be
Babies lying in their cages, free
Some mommies want me, so she say
Some grandmas want me equally
Man who talk so sweet to me
Come, child, Katie

Come, child, Katie
Cockroach Katie
Maybe paradise has never been
Come, child, Katie
Maybe, maybe
There's a pseudo saint out there

Excuse me, sorry
Go I may
So much dirty clothes today
My wagon, pretty, four new wheels
I so proud
Is good I feel
But so much laundry
Black and red
I see those colors in my head...

There's a window by the stair
There's some sunlight way out there
I've heard it's warm
Or so it's said
But in the context of your days
That seems so far away

What Neverland your home must be
Come, child, Katie

Come, child, Katie
Cockroach Katie
Maybe paradise has never been
Come, child, Katie
Maybe, maybe
There's a pseudo saint out there
    1-15-93/1995

THOUGH I HAD NEARLY FORGOTTEN YOU – the poem

There's a wind beneath the breeze
There's a light beneath the sun
There are toasted shreds of summer leaves
Beneath the sleepy northwest trees
There are memories
Left behind so easily
That have now all come back
Though I had nearly forgotten you
Yeh, we were once boys, and then we were men

There's a smile beneath my eyes
The old rhythm's in my step
There's a funny way the clown in us cries
When he can't do what he longs to try
There are footsteps near
Their time, the tune you left to them
It'll weave a funny pattern
Because of what I learned today
Though it's been years since I'd thought of you
Heh, we were once boys, and then we were men
Here stands a band of boys and men
Understudies, solo roles
In solitude each one
And each one, up here,
Will go ahead and take his bow
Then take the roses
That as of now are meant for you
Then go home
Once boys
Then men

There's the earth beneath the ground
And a sadness in the sound
Disharmony
In what I'll sing
Beneath your sleeping skies tonight
With silence all around

If I'm really all alone
Then why do I feel you near
When I just heard the news
Though I had nearly forgotten you
Once we were boys, and now we are just men

5-9/10-92

THOUGH I HAD NEARLY FORGOTTEN YOU – the song

There's a wind beneath the breeze
There are toasted shreds of summer leaves
There's a fading light beneath the sun
There are memories
Left behind so easily
They've all come back one by one

Because of news I heard of you
Though I had nearly forgotten you

There's a smile beneath my eyes
It's a funny thing to see me cry
Some rhythm's there as I walk by
There are footsteps
In time the way you left them
They'll weave an inconsistent pattern

Because of news I heard of you
Though I had nearly forgotten you

So go ahead and take the roses
You know they're meant for you
Go ahead and take the roses
Though I had nearly forgotten you

There's the earth beneath the ground
And a sadness in the song
Disharmony, the sound is wrong
With steadfast silence all around
And if I'm really all alone
Why had I forgotten you?

What echoes should I want to hear
What wisdom lingers far from here
Is your memory your gift
Though I'd forgotten you?

The differences that made us laugh
The whimsical, the circumstance
The different roads, the crazy paths
The questions we forgot to ask
The miles between our childhood lives
The ages in the old man's smile
I'm sorry I'd forgotten you
I'm sorry I'd forgotten you

1994

IT'S OK – the poem

Hey man, I said
I don't know
If I want to know
Anymore about that crap
I've been around before
My head's still reelin'
And I'm still feelin'
The cold and emptiness
Of a lost-love aftershock
I don't know
If I want to know…

It's OK to love again
It's OK to love again…

Shut up, I said
I don't know
If I want to know
The way the story ends
I thought I knew the rules
Oh, Lord, who'd ever know
What kind of fool
I'd find way down inside
Once I'd found the courage
To look
Why should I want to know…

It's OK to love again
It's OK to love again…

Oh no, it's not
(It's OK to love again)
Oh, God, it hurts way too much
(It's OK to love again)
But she intoxicates
(It's like smooth wine; it's not poison)
My spirit feels her warmth

(You can touch her kind of sun)
Do you know I want to kiss her?
(A sweeter piece of wisdom)
But, God, what if I fall in love?

It's OK to love again
It's OK to love again…

2-17-93

IT'S OK – the song

KimAnn I said
I don't know if I want to know
The way you feel
Or where you go
Cuz I'm still reeling
And I'm still feeling
The cold and emptiness
Of a lost love aftershock

Oh no
I don't know if I want to know
I don't want to know
Anymore

Is it OK to love again?
Is it OK to love again?
I don't trust anybody
      (I don't trust you)
I don't need anybody
      (I don't need you)
But I don't want to be alone

Inside myself
I can't find the words to say
The songs to sing
Or anything
I've locked myself into
A castle I built with you
The halls are tall and wide
And I'm alone inside

Oh no
I don't know if I want to know
I don't want to know
Oh

Is it OK to love again?

Is it OK to love again?
I don't trust anybody
      (I don't trust you)
I don't need anybody
      (I don't need you)
But I don't want to be alone

KimAnn I said
Do you know if you want to know
The way I feel
Or where I go?

I'm still reeling
I'm still feeling
The cold and emptiness
Of a lost-love aftershock

You don't want to know
I know you don't want to know
Don't want to know
Anymore

Lyrics revisions by Michael L. Schultz
1993

LADDERS

I see you're tired
I sense your weariness
I know you need your peace tonight
I know you want to rest

This life is rough
Our goals become steeper
And, yes, we've come far
But there's oh, so far to go

Sometimes I sit
At night, all by myself
I wish you'd sit with me a while
Halfway met is hard to find

There will always be ladders
Climbers we'll always be
Let's not lose sight of the ground
As we help each other up
There will always be ladders
As fare as we can see
On we climb
Never quite free
Held by bonds
And promises

1991

NOBLE LITTLE SOLDIER

Noble little soldier
Wants me to say, "I love him"
Purest little anger
Rising from the ashes
Of what used to be
For him
For me

Noble little soldier
He looks out on this world
Hardened little heart
Sees in shades grown colder
Holds one precious wish
"Love her"
"Love him"

Life rearranges
Love's definition
Changes, changes
What used to be
We'll hold precious, dear
And keep moving on from here
Hold precious, dear
Keep moving on from here

I love you, little soldier
But it's something I can't do
I know how much you love him
But, soldier, there's someone new
Someone's come to love me
And he's falling in love with you
Someone's come to love me
And he's falling in love with you

Noble little soldier
Noble little soldier
Noble little soldier….

2-93

THE PENDULUM IS RISING

I looked over both shoulders today
I looked to the man on his knees east
I looked to the weary merchant's west
I looked over my cup of black coffee

Contemplated the best
Saw fragments of the past
Back and forth was once enough
The pendulum is rising

I'm scaling jagged ancient crags
Icy daggers rake my fingertips
Himalayan winds brush against my swollen lips
A blinding light reflects against my nomad's eye

And if I fell a part of me has wondered still
How it would feel to feel the freedom of a fall
Heaven bent
Heaven sent
The pendulum is rising

I recognize the choices made
The anvil forged and the bricks were laid
I carved the stone, the iron bent
Make my will my own, damn it

Confusion in the chaos
Resolution amid peace
The savages still shout
And I still want to listen

I am the well-meant warrior
Bent on finding the better way
I am the climber
I am the flyer

I wonder at the feeling

Wonder at the falling
I see the moment swaying
The pendulum is rising

1995

ART

If the darkness pulls at you
And you reach between the lines
If the falter in the moment
Sends a picture to your mind

And the words, they seem to alter
And change into mere lies
Then the truth is lost and far behind
By the broken and the unread signs

When questions are the answer
Though you turn your eyes away
The memory is burned inside
And the images are grave
The images are grave

When little more is left
And scattered is the rest
Idiots and imbeciles sleep warm tonight
And slowly start to die

And the poets are the paupers
And the art is kept alive

Look at you
Look at me
In what we've done just say, "Believe!"
Look way beyond
Look deep within
See the fantasy begin

Look at me
Look at you
It's a crooked, painful kind of truth
It's bitter fruit
It's blood red juice

The poets drink 'til it's gone
And paupers want this martyrdom
While simple people slowly die
So long as Art is kept alive
So long as Art is kept alive
So long as Art is kept
Alive

1995

WORDS

And she handed her a book
With maps and violets laid to rest
Between each torn and blistered little scrap
Words and colors bled to one
Pens and tears and then some
She handed her a book
And she said,

"This is what you asked for
When you said that it was over
This is why you cried when it was over
This is what you cried for
Though you didn't know it
This is why you cried when it was over."

The heat in its spine
Tingling, burning a symbol
Into the writer's tired, folded hands
Something whispered of hieroglyphs
The woman's voice
The seraphim
The words from somewhere no one dared to ask

"This is what you asked for
When you said that it was over
This is why you cried when it was over
This is what you cried for
Though you didn't know it
This is why you cried when it was over."

This is what Pandora's box
Kept cold for you
And these are the arctic, arid skies
That hold a shooting star death
This is the aurora
That danced before your disbelieving eyes

"This is what you asked for
When you said that it was over
This is why you cried when it was over
This is what you cried for
Though you didn't know it
This is why you cried when it was over."

12-7-93/2005

SLEEPLESS

Save this hour for the sleepless
Whisper one forbidden question
Are the bells still ringing soulful
When there's no one left to listen?

Who is left to hear
Who's left to hold when you're alone
Is solitude and freedom?
Is solitude a prison?

Save this hour for the sleepless
Don't build a temple to yourself
Who'd be left to hear your prayers
And who'd be left to sing?

Is there no one near
Unearthly quiet holds no peace
Who's ever lived in paradise?
Are we here to fantasize?

Save the hour for the sleepless
When your muse is calling to you
What does she try to whisper
And can you even hear her?

Is this why you're still awake
Is this why you're so far away
Is this where you want to stay
Is there nothing I can say?

1993/1995

TONIGHT I'LL BE IN HEAVEN

My mother, oh, my father
I heard about an angel
The kind that has no wings

Is it love that cuts the ribbon
Is it hate that breaks the rythm
I have no fear
No, no keep to yourself your tears
Tonight I'll be in heaven

My mother, oh, my father
I heard about an angel
The kind that has no wings

The bread is not my manna
My soul is lost in famine
Now it's searching for a home
Perhaps he's waiting for me there
Where the light consumes forever

My mother, oh my father
I promise I'm not damned
I heard about an angel
The kind that bears all sadness
The kind that never sings
When everything is not enough
The longing that it brings
Tonight I'll be in heaven
Heaven....

I heard about an angel
Who lost the one love she had found
The crimson flowers on her gown
Were woven in his blood

Perhaps he's waiting for me
Perhaps he's waiting for me there

I have no tears
No, no keep to yourself your fears

1993/1995

EARTHBOUND ETHEREAL

There comes a time
When the release
Isn't borne of pain or fear
The obligation to appease
When circumstance
Washes away
The fragments of all that once was
And is no longer

Letting go
Can be so hard
What is right
Is right
Forget the question
Trust your reflection
The mirror I now hold out
Before you

Ethereal
Ethereal
Comes a time when the earthbound fly

It's all okay
It will be wonderful
If it leaves us sleepless
So be it
Let it be
Let's heed the self-same energy
That called a faith-filled heart to beat
And led
At long, long last
You to me

Now intertwined
It's justified
And breathes on through
A someone, someone new

This is why we are alive
This is the sign we seek
This is the rhyme
These are the wings
That make
The earthbound fly

Ethereal
Ethereal
These make the earthbound fly
        2/2011

BEAUTIFUL RAGE - preliminary draft

Beautiful rage
Paints in painful, primal colors
Shards soar beyond what others call
Sweet love
Or lust
Or poisoned sonnets
Impassioned rants
Who feeds off sex
When rage is there to bend in half
Backwards
Inside out
Oh,
Backwards
Inside out
It's as bitter as it's fucking sweet
Three verses
Bridge
Repeat, repeat
Oh, Come
Come to me now
Oh, Come
Come with me now

It's the storm and the desire
It's agony, it's ecstasy
The darkest corners of the wayward mind
Illuminate the midnight
Each secret pulls me
Down, down, down
Each secret pulls me down

Oh,
Backwards
Inside out
It's as bitter as it's fucking sweet
Three verses
Bridge

Repeat, repeat
Oh, Come
Come to me now
Oh, come
Come with me now

1-22/23-2012

BEAUTIFUL RAGE - draft with coda

Beautiful rage
Paints in painful, primal colors
Shards soar beyond what others call
Sweet love
Or lust
Or poisoned sonnets
Impassioned rants
Who feeds off sex
When rage is there to bend in half
Backwards
Inside out
Oh,
Backwards
Inside out
It's as bitter as it's fucking sweet
Three verses
Bridge
Repeat, repeat
Oh, come to me now
Oh, come with me now
Oh, come to me now
Oh, come with me now

It's the storm and the desire
It's agony, it's ecstasy
The darkest corners of the wayward mind
Illuminate the midnight
Each secret pulls me
Down, down, down
Each secret pulls me down

Beautiful rage
Inspiration's unfit mother
Who needs conventionality
When gods
And ghosts
In dark hours call me

Impassioned rants
Who suffers less
When works are there to bend in half

Oh,
Backwards
Inside out
It's as bitter as it's fucking sweet
Three verses
Bridge
Repeat, repeat
Oh, come to me now
Oh, come with me now
Oh, come to me now
Oh, come with me now

It's the pain in understanding
Acceptance of the hand of Time
The apple and the serpent work as one
The knowledge I am left with
The words that do not leave me
Each mem'ry pulls me
Down, down, down
Each mem'ry pulls me
Down, down, down

It's agony
It's ecstasy
It's words wrapped in
Charred melodies
It's every storm
And all desire
When madness feeds
Impassioned fires
It's poisoned anthems
It's toxic odes
It's secrets borne
Of ages old
It's blinding light

And shattered eyes
When truth lays bare
The futile trial
And casts it to
Indiff'rent winds
So soon it's lost
Begin again

It's silence filled with voices
Enjoined and intertwined
A soul that's speaking from a beating heart
That sees celestial rhythm
And reads in dying stars
A song that takes me
Down, down, down
A song that takes me
Down, down, down
A song that takes me
Down, down, down...

1-27/30, 2-20-2012
Available on YouTube

www.ingramcontent.com/pod-product-compliance
Lightning Source LLC
LaVergne TN
LVHW051514070426
835507LV00023B/3111